Solidarity Betrayed

"Ava Avendaño's book is a clarion call to justice, marrying vivid survivors' stories with her incisive legal and cultural critique. This accessible and transformative book urges readers to envision a world rooted in dignity and collective resistance."

—Soraya Chemaly, author of *Rage Becomes Her: The Power of Women's Anger*

"An important and courageous book that shines an informed light on the failure of certain unions and leaders to respond to sexual harassment and the resulting damage to those victimized and the movement more generally."

—William A. Herbert, Distinguished Lecturer, Hunter College, City University of New York

"*Solidarity Betrayed* is a courageous masterwork of reporting and analysis that gives voice to those who have suffered sexual abuse in the workplace and sheds light on those workers who have managed to redress imbalances of power that keep victims quiet and perpetrators free. It is a must-read for anyone who loves our country's labor movement and dreams of a future without sexual violence at work."

—Greg Asbed, Coalition of Immokalee Workers

Solidarity Betrayed

How Unions Enable Sexual Harassment—And How They Can Do Better

Ana Avendaño

First published 2025 by Pluto Press
New Wing, Somerset House, Strand, London WC2R 1LA
and Pluto Press, Inc.
1930 Village Center Circle, 3-834, Las Vegas, NV 89134

www.plutobooks.com

British Library Cataloguing in Publication Data
A catalogue record for this book is available from the British Library

ISBN 978 0 7453 4906 0   Paperback
ISBN 978 0 7453 4918 3   PDF
ISBN 978 0 7453 4917 6   EPUB

This book is printed on paper suitable for recycling and made from fully
managed and sustained forest sources. Logging, pulping and manufacturing
processes are expected to conform to the environmental standards of the
country of origin.

Typeset by Stanford DTP Services, Northampton, England

Simultaneously printed in the United Kingdom and United States of America

Contents

To Gersio, who will live in my heart forever. *Ni una sola nube.*

Acknowledgements

I extend my deepest gratitude to the incredible people who have supported me throughout this journey: Paula Brantner, Arcy Reilly-Collins, Linda Seabrook, Sara Wilder, Roxanne Rife, Alejandra Valles, Sandra Diaz, KC Wagner, Alice Heiserman, Jon Hiatt, Katy Fox-Hodess, Suzette Wright, Rocky Kabir, Lois Jenson, Lisa Heap, Barbro Budin, Sanjay Pinto, and Emily Williams—thank you for your unwavering support, insightful feedback, and encouragement. Each of you has played a vital role in bringing this book to life. Your belief in my vision and your contributions have made this work possible. I am truly grateful to have such a remarkable network of friends and colleagues. I also thank all the women who trusted me with their private stories; when you are ready to share openly, I promise I will be there to support you.

Introduction

This book is a "tough love" letter to the labor movement. Unions are the most powerful institutions on the side of working people. They were established to promote dignity, equality, and respect for all workers. As such, unions have an essential role to play in creating safer and more supportive and accountable workplaces. Yet, they have failed to address one of the most harmful, dehumanizing aspects of the workplace: sexual harassment. When it comes to a member sexually harassing another—or labor leaders harassing their staff—unions deploy the mechanisms of protection to defend harassers, leaving the victims feeling betrayed and marginalized. The masculinist, sometimes brutal culture on which unions were built remains very much alive today.

Sexual harassment is nothing new. In January 1976, *Redbook* magazine invited its readers to respond to a questionnaire titled "How Do You Handle Sex on the Job?"—a cringe-inducing description of sexual harassment by today's standards. The magazine published the results in a bluntly titled article, "What men do to women on the job: A shocking look at sexual harassment."[1] Nine thousand women filled out the questionnaire by hand and mailed it in. More than 8000 of them (92 percent) said that sexual harassment at work was a problem, with a majority of those who responded saying it was "a serious one."[2]

Fast forward 40 years, and things don't seem to have changed all that much. *Redbook* asked readers to take the same survey in 2016 with one minor adjustment. Eighty percent of those who responded have experienced sexual harassment at work.[3] According to a survey by Women in Film, five years after #MeToo, 70 percent of respondents said the industry's culture of abuse and misconduct had "improved somewhat," but 69 percent said they had experienced abuse or misconduct within that time frame.[4]

Official government statistics paint an equally bleak picture. Between 25 and 85 percent of women, depending on how you ask the question, in U.S. workplaces experience some form of sexual harassment, according to the U.S. Equal Employment Opportunity Commission (EEOC), the federal agency responsible for enforcing laws that prohibit discrimination in the workplace.[5]

Change is most surely necessary, but it requires confronting painful truths. I learned this difficult lesson when I was fired for exposing sexual harassment in 2019. I had been in the labor movement for more than two decades as a labor lawyer and as senior staff to the president of the AFL-CIO, the national umbrella for unions in the United States.

In 2019, I served as vice president for Labor Engagement at United Way Worldwide, the headquarters of one of the largest charities in the world. I managed a program with its roots in World War II, through which local United Way branches receive funding from union members directly through their paychecks—a system similar to how union members pay their union dues. The local United Ways employ men and women to serve as labor liaisons—working with local unions to convince union members to donate to the charity. When they are not fundraising, they serve as staff to the local labor councils where they are often housed.

A couple of years before my ouster, I learned that union leaders were sexually harassing female labor liaisons. I received a report that a young woman from Florida resigned after being sexually harassed by a labor leader who sat on the board of the local labor council where the woman's office was located. The harasser had power over this young woman; she needed his support to do her job (raise funds from local union members). He invited her to drinks, commented on her clothes, and touched her inappropriately. This behavior went on for months. When she reported him to her United Way supervisor, she was told to work remotely. The labor council president (her other boss) did not like that suggestion; she wanted her on-site. When the liaison pressed the issue, the labor council president, an older woman who had been around for decades, accused the young liaison of having an affair with the harasser and posted negative comments about her on Facebook.

I was appalled. I called all the labor liaisons together on a call to assure them that sexual harassment was utterly unacceptable, whether perpetrated by a labor leader, United Way employee, or a donor. I soon heard from other liaisons that they, too, had experienced sexual harassment at the hands of labor leaders but had not come forward for fear of retaliation and losing their jobs.

One liaison had been forced by her boss to watch pornography while working at the union food shelter. Several women reported that men cat-called and groped them when they visited job sites. And one courageous liaison, Sara Wilder, reported abuse that spanned years. Sara shares her story later in the book.

I immediately contacted Al Davidoff, who served as the national point person for the project. He was skeptical at first and then dismissive: "Sounds like a cranky labor leader," he told me. He and other senior staff insisted that there was nothing they could do because the labor council president and the harasser were not their employees. This, even though the national AFL-CIO wields enormous control over the local labor councils: it funds them, sets standards on what they can and cannot do programmatically and with regard to electoral endorsements, and controls various other important functions.

A few months later, I invited the AFL-CIO to join us in a crowdsourcing project with the well-respected non-profit organization Futures Without Violence. We would collect answers to the question, "How can we help women (especially union staff and leaders and women who work closely with unions) feel safe from harassment or physical assaults at work and work-related spaces?" The AFL-CIO declined.

It became clear to me that the AFL-CIO would not help the liaisons, so I shifted my program resources to address the problem. I co-hosted conferences with Futures Without Violence on sexual harassment. I brought in an officer from the Canadian Labor Congress (the Canadian equivalent of the AFL-CIO) to share what Canadian unions were doing to address the problem. She told us they had developed a code of conduct for union leaders and staff across the country, which was a helpful tool. I shared that with the national AFL-CIO and heard nothing for almost a year, when they adopted the code to much internal fanfare and self-congratulation.

Meanwhile, in August 2017, my program hosted a conference in Portland, Oregon. One of the main plenary sessions featured Sara Wilder, the liaison from Kansas who shares her painful story in Chapter 3.

The panel also featured Karen Kent, the president of UNITE HERE Local 1 in Chicago, who pioneered a campaign to protect hotel housekeepers from sexual harassment by hotel guests, as well as Bob Reiter, the then-second in command (now the leader) of the Chicago Federation of Labor.

Kent shared stories of her members and the union's efforts. Reiter, a former employment lawyer, talked about the shortcomings of addressing sexual harassment through lawsuits and the power that unions had to change systems of abuse. They sent a powerful message: harassment is a union issue. Several liaisons in the audience stood up to share their powerful stories, some in tears. We left the conference hoping that a shift in how unions address sexual harassment was coming.

Two months later, the #MeToo movement went viral.

A few weeks after that, several media outlets exposed senior union staff and leaders as sexual harassers. Scott Courtney, the architect of the Service Employees International Union's (SEIU) Fight for $15 campaign, along with several lower staffers, were fired or resigned after press reports of their long history of demanding sexual favors from female staffers.[6] The AFL-CIO's chief budget officer, Terry Stapleton, was permitted to resign on the eve of the publication of a press story that he had sent lewd text messages to a secretary and pressed her to come to his hotel room. American Federation of Teachers (AFT) president Randi Weingarten said in a statement following that revelation,

You can't talk the talk of civil rights and economic dignity without walking the walk. Unions, more than most, must understand that lesson, and we must do everything we can to ensure our workplaces are free from sexual harassment. That means, just as we criticized [Donald] Trump and [Harvey] Weinstein and [Roger] Ailes, we must have zero tolerance for sexual harassment in our own house. Creating a clear and effective policy remedying sexual harassment is

an important first step for the AFL-CIO, but it's not suffi-
cient. The AFL-CIO should lead, not follow, when it comes
to workplace safety, which means not just reacting but
creating an anti-harassment culture. Working women and
their families must be able to have confidence and trust in
their unions.[7]

Yet, the AFL-CIO did little more than talk the talk. The
former and current presidents of the AFL-CIO (Rich Trumka
and Liz Shuler) issued a statement that deflected accountability for having kept a sexual harasser on senior staff and, at the
same time, acknowledged that the institution needs to take
action:

The recent news regarding sexual harassment in numerous
industries has shown that no organization, including our
own, is immune to a culture that has allowed both women
and men to feel unsafe and threatened on the job ... as the
premier organization for working people, we recognize that
we bear a special responsibility to lead by our actions and
example.[8]

A few months later, together with Linda Seabrook, then-
General Counsel for Futures Without Violence, and KC
Wagner of Cornell University's Worker Institute, I hosted a
plenary session on unions and sexual harassment at United
Way. We talked about the need for labor unions to tackle the
issue of harassment and gave concrete examples of how that
can be done. In my remarks, I spoke about Terry Stapleton
(with whom I worked for years at the AFL-CIO), what he had
done, and how important it is for men in powerful positions
to be held accountable. I noted that he had not been held

accountable. Instead, he had landed a cushy job at a charity that sells child identification toolkits to unions—so that parents can prevent their kids from being abducted. Not surprisingly, the head of the child identification organization was close to AFL-CIO then-president Rich Trumka.

Three hours after the session ended, I received a phone call instructing me to make an appointment to meet with the CEO of United Way, Brian Gallagher. I met with him the next day. That meeting blew my mind. Within those three hours, Rich Trumka had called Gallagher, furious. As Gallagher explained, Trumka told him that I had "defamed good guys who had passed through his shop" and "got caught up in the #MeToo stuff." Gallagher also told me that Trumka was unhappy that I had called one of those "good guys" "a pedophile." When Gallagher asked me if that was true, I told him that I never used the term "pedophile" because, well, I know what pedophile means. Gallagher also said that Trumka was upset about the title of the plenary ("Sexual Harassment and the Labor Movement"). When Gallagher told me that, I shrugged my shoulders in confusion. Gallagher did the same.

As it turns out, a female AFL-CIO staffer, Yael Foa, had been in the audience during the plenary; she sent her notes to her female boss, Prairie Wells, who then contacted Paul Lemmon, Trumka's chief enforcer. Foa's notes landed on Trumka's desk shortly after that. As bell hooks reminds us, "patriarchy has no gender."[9] Women and men alike can be complicit in perpetuating oppression.

A few months later, after I published two articles on the labor movement's failure to adequately address sexual harassment, I was falsely accused of bullying my staff and ousted from my job.

Being fired can be a devastating blow. It's like being stripped of a part of your identity, as if your contributions and dedication have suddenly been invalidated. I found my footing with the help of an incredible strategic and supportive lawyer, Carla Brown. We sued and won a substantial settlement.

Several women came forward claiming discrimination after I left, which the *Huffington Post* publicized in a series of articles.[10] As of February 3, 2021, Brian Gallagher was no longer the CEO of United Way. He received $3,180,985 as compensation when he left.[11]

My fight is larger than myself and what happened to me. The point is that the problem is continuing, and we need to alert people to the reality that impacts so many others.

I am a strong union supporter. I know the labor movement is messy and full of contradictions; it's a work in progress. I also know that unions can do better.

As I was getting my bearings following these events, I read everything I could get my hands on about the labor movement's relationship with sexual harassment. I spoke with women who had been harassed and sought their union's help only to be told, sorry, no can do. I spoke with academics, lawyers, and activists who had dealt with unions' failures to address harassment. They warned me that I was getting into dangerous waters. I knew that already, given that the patriarchy had taken my job. Nonetheless, I was naive.

I still believed that the labor movement as a whole was so much more than a few old-school bad apples. Until then, my career had focused on immigrant workers, and leveraging the power of the institution to change the laws and practices that oppressed workers.

Dealing with harassment was completely different. It was about challenging the patriarchal power that kept men in positions at the top of the labor hierarchy. It was about challenging the identity of labor leaders. It was about challenging a masculinist and sexist culture that has served men well for centuries.

The women who warned me about the danger of going down this road were right. Unions were not willing to look inward. Instead, they went into full armadillo mode, toughening their shell and protecting their soft underbelly.

Early on in my career as a union lawyer, a sweet older man—a director at the United Food and Commercial Workers Union where I worked at the time—gave me a warning that would become all too real decades later. He told me to be careful because when they can't challenge your competency, they'll challenge your loyalty.

The *Huffington Post* published an article that included my story along with the stories of other women who had suffered harassment and discrimination at United Way in 2020.[12] I posted the article on the Facebook page of the Union Leadership Academy, a University of Massachusetts at Amherst Masters Program I was attending. Within hours, it was taken down. I later learned that three local union leaders had contacted the program director, demanding that it be taken down. How fragile must an institutional ego be to be threatened by a Facebook post?

The AFL-CIO disinvited me from a meeting that it hosted with the chair of the EEOC and union presidents on the topic of sexual harassment. A friend told me that my name was scratched off the invite list by Paul Lemmon.

I also learned that a pamphlet that Linda Seabrook and I had written called "Top 10 things unions can do right now to address sexual harassment in the workplace"[13] had been removed from packets that were to be distributed at the meeting because the pamphlet did not pass legal review.

According to my source, an AFL-CIO lawyer told her that our contention that "victims should be believed and respected" was not legally sound. Of course, we weren't instructing union members, educators, stewards, and leaders on evidentiary standards; we were simply urging them to give victims their due dignity.

In the pages that follow, you will see that women faced hard times in the early history of organized labor. They were excluded and marginalized by male trade unionists, yet they forged their path forward. As women entered the workforce in larger numbers in the late 1960s and 1970s and dared to work in jobs that had been traditionally reserved for men, they were met with resistance and vituperation. Men used sexual harassment as a tool to keep women out and remind them that they were inferior. Unions played along, to different degrees. But it was women, through their own strength, humor, and creativity, who found a way forward.

You will also hear the present-day experiences of women (and a man) who were sexually harassed and then betrayed by their unions—often because the harasser was a union man. Their painful stories make clear that unions continue to act as if we are living in the 1950s, where women are encouraged to be agreeable, avoid confrontation, and refrain from challenging established systems or male authority figures.

This problem is more than just hypocrisy; it is a threat to the movement. More than half of workers are women, and the institution that relies on workers for its very existence cannot simply shrug its shoulders in the face of a degrading, ubiquitous practice.

You will also see in the pages that follow that enablers come in various guises. Labor law plays a large role in creating cultures that reflect the worst of masculinity, not only juvenile but sometimes violent and vicious. Unions use anachronistic legal constructs to defend harassers at the expense of victims, and they continue to defend practices that are sexist, misogynistic, and embarrassing.

One of the anecdotes I shared in the piece I published in the wake of #MeToo referred to the Union Sportsmen Alliance, an antidote to the National Rifle Association that unions formed in 2007. For years, the AFL-CIO hosted an annual fundraiser at its headquarters, which consisted of an upscale, catered cocktail party and gun show. Very tall and extremely thin women in identical micro mini-skirts and 5-inch heels serve as hostesses. Several of us complained to the President's Office that the event was degrading to women and offensive. Trumka told his assistants that our views were classist.

Some women in power have made an important difference. Alejandra Valles and Sandra Diaz, Latina, elected leaders of the janitors' union in California, United Service Workers West (USWW), believed in the power of their members to lead internal change that made their union the shining example of how unions should be using their power to eradicate sexual harassment. Through innovative peer-led member education, partnerships with civil rights and anti-rape organizations, lobbying and other legislative efforts, and the collective bargaining process, the union created a powerful blueprint for the kind of real-world progress that unions can achieve when they fully commit their resources to efforts led by sexual assault survivors and immigrant women of color. You'll hear more about their efforts in Chapter 5.

Karen Kent, the Chicago UNITE-HERE president, also made a difference. Yet, what is also clear is that having more women in leadership positions does not automatically bring change. In the labor movement, high-ranking women—who are almost always white—serve as gatekeepers much more often than they serve as sisters in the struggle. Mary Kay Henry (then- president of the SEIU) was Scott Courtney's (one of the highest-ranking union officials outed by #MeToo) boss for more than a decade while he abused the women he supervised. Liz Shuler was the second in command at the AFL-CIO while Terry Stapleton sexually harassed his secretary. Labor feminism needs a refresh. The pages that follow will explore these themes in more detail.

Unions play a promising role in global efforts to eliminate harassment in the world of work. The problems documented here are not exclusive to the United States, as you will learn in Chapter 6. British, African, and other countries' trade unions have been rocked by scandal. At the same time, unions are pushing their governments to adopt anti-sexual harassment laws, and educating their members on how to deal with harassment. The International Trade Union Confederation (ITUC) brought workers' voices and experiences to the table at the International Labour Organization and together with many activists and non-governmental organizations (NGOs) won the first convention that addresses gender-based violence at work, including sexual harassment: 44 countries ratified that convention within the first five years, with Uruguay, Argentina, Ecuador, Fiji, Namibia and Somalia leading the pack.[14]

I have written this book in the hope that women who were betrayed by their unions will find solace in knowing that they are not alone and that unions that continue to defend harassers at all costs and cling to destructive masculinist practices will see that change is not only possible but necessary. Together, we can make a difference.

1

In the Course of History

I have a great bone to pick with the organized labor movement. They are the greatest offender as far as discrimination against women is concerned.

—Bessie Abramowitz Hillman, founder of the
Amalgamated Clothing Workers of America, 1961[1]

The early history of the American labor movement centers on men: the early leaders, the rebels, and the visionaries—all men. Yet, as early as 1825, American women were organizing for economic demands, even though they were excluded from most unions.[2] In the small number of unions that permitted both men and women as members, it was not uncommon for women to take the lead in militant actions. As the historian Alice Kessler-Harris has documented, in 1899, during a strike of Iowa cigar makers, some men returned to work while the women remained steadfast, exemplifying their resilience and determination.[3] Similarly, in 1905, boot and shoemakers in Massachusetts were renowned for their unwavering negotiation tactics. Their union president recognized that "It is harder to induce women to compromise ... they are more likely to hold out to the bitter end ... to obtain exactly what they want."[4] Women's tenacity was not limited to defying the boss but also their union. Polish textile workers in Massachusetts stood fast against the employer cutting their rate of pay, despite the union's advice that they arbitrate the matter—and won a resounding victory.

Not surprisingly, in the early 1900s, women in a variety of occupations—including garment workers, tobacco strippers, and telephone operators from California to Massachusetts—ran highly successful women-only unions. Women also built a revolutionary union of domestic workers through the Industrial Workers of the World (IWW).[5]

Later, in the 1970s, as the labor movement was in steep decline, women accounted for almost all of the new union membership. Some of the most inspirational and energetic organizing campaigns are the product of women's creativity and struggles—from the iconic Bread and Roses strike in the Massachusetts textile mills of the early 1900s to the graduate student organizing today.

Women trade unionists who fought for equality and fairness and against the greed of the bosses lived in a world where women were second-class citizens.

The enduring ideology that has justified the exclusion of women from labor markets is generally: (1) Women belong in the home, not in the workplace; they should not be rewarded financially for abandoning their natural role; (2) Women are unskilled workers. Their jobs don't require training or experience; (3) Women don't deserve to make as much money as men; (4) Women don't take work seriously; (5) Women can't be trusted to take on the hard work of the labor movement; (6) Women are in the workforce temporarily, only until they find a husband.[6]

This ideology undergirded the exclusion of women from unions. According to Samuel Gompers, the first president of the American Federation of Labor, "It is the so-called competition of the unorganized defenseless woman worker, the girl, and the wife, that often tends to reduce the wages of the father and husband."[7] Not surprisingly, of the 13 founding unions of

14

the American Federation of Labor (AFL), only two, the Typographical Union and Cigar Makers, admitted women.[8]

By the late 1890s, most AFL national affiliates amended their constitutions to allow for female membership but found ways to keep women out. Common methods included high initiation fees and restrictive apprenticeship programs. The Molders Union charged a $55 fine to any member who instructed women in the trade.[9]

A more nuanced approach was to call for wage equality for women, "equal compensation for equal services performed," which, as labor men well knew, was a way to deprive women of jobs because no employer would prefer a woman over a man for the same wage.[10] Another way that union men restricted women's ability to work was by advocating for protective legislation that restricted the hours that women could work and the types of jobs they could perform.[11] Those laws, which were upheld (and later set aside) by the Supreme Court, showed a "romantic paternalism, which in practical effect, put women not on a pedestal, but in a cage."[12]

Even when women organized themselves, the established labor movement denied them recognition. In the early 1900s, women printers in New York, candy workers in Philadelphia, hairdressers in Seattle, and streetcar conductors in Cleveland organized and petitioned for a charter that would formally recognize them as affiliates of the AFL. The AFL turned them down.

Nor did the AFL stand by women workers following World War I or World War II, when women entered the workforce in large numbers. Following World War II, organized labor participated in a cultural and legal consensus that married women belonged in the home and that they should leave their jobs in the hands of returning veterans.[13] Thus, women were displaced, with little government support or labor support. Both federations, the AFL and the Congress of Industrial Organizations (CIO) were absent.

Worse, unions sanctioned discrimination against women through collective bargaining. Several unions bargained for prohibitions against the employment of married women. Others agreed to the discharge of single women who married. Yet others bargained for unequal hiring of, and wage rates for, men and women doing similar jobs where lower-paying jobs were given to women.[14]

Well into the 1960s and 1970s, unions sided with employers on matters that benefited men at the expense of women workers, especially women of color. Those included protective measures like weight lifting restrictions, hours limitations, and separate jobs for men and women.[15] The International Longshore and Warehouse Union (ILWU) maintained a provision in its contract that allowed the "son of an active deceased longshoreman" the right to join the union by "taking his father's union book"—a provision that remained until the 1970s when a southern Californian female dock worker sued the union.[16]

Labor leaders also fought vehemently to lessen liability for themselves under the Civil Rights Act of 1964, which, for the first time, made workplace discrimination on the basis of race, gender, and ethnicity unlawful. They did so by trying to weaken the Equal Employment Opportunity Commission (EEOC), the government agency charged with enforcing the law, and diverting claims away from the courts to the EEOC for both gender and race.[17] Some unions pushed the EEOC to interpret the legal term "bona fide occupational qualifications" in a very broad way.[18] This expansive interpretation would create a loophole, allowing employers and unions to continue discriminating based on gender and race, even though anti-discrimination laws were in place. Essentially, these unions were trying to maintain certain discriminatory practices by exploiting a technicality in the law.

Women's history in the labor movement evolved along labor markets that remain highly segmented by gender and race. Four in ten women work in female-dominated occupations (where women make up at least 75 percent of the labor force), and only 5.5 percent of all women work in male-dominated occupations, where the pay is better, benefits are more plentiful, and chances for advancement abound.[19]

The gender composition of unions, particularly those that are occupationally based, is related to labor market gender segmentation. Some unions represent overwhelmingly male constituencies: the building trades, pilots, and firefighters, to name a few.[20] Other unions, namely, teachers' and nurses' unions, have large female memberships.

Unions organized around industrial lines like auto and steel also tend to be male-dominated. As the sociologist Ruth Milkman explains, "In the twenty-first century, the typical male union member is a private-sector, blue-collar 'hardhat,' whereas the typical female union member is a public-sector, white-collar or professional worker employed in education, health-care, or public administration."[21]

LABOR'S LEGACY OF FAILURE TO PROTECT WOMEN

The 1970s brought radical opportunities and enormous challenges for working women. The Civil Rights Act required that jobs that had once been the province of men be open to women. For the first time, women could earn a decent wage and hold a job that offered security and benefits.

As they entered the workforce in record numbers, women quickly began to challenge workplace norms, especially in occupations that had been reserved for men. Those jobs—in construction sites, firehouses, auto manufacturing plants, mines from Minnesota to Tennessee, and many others—paid the highest wages and often came with a union card.

In 1974, the EEOC and several mining companies entered into a consent decree that guaranteed that 20 percent of jobs in production and maintenance would be set aside for women and racial minorities.[22] Women faced difficult, often brutal, and sometimes violent conditions. In coal mines, they faced a strong fraternal culture built on generations of men working together in dangerous conditions and a long-held superstition that women were bad luck in the mines. When forced to admit women into the mines by the courts and the government, the men in some places brought back an initiation rite where miners would strip and grease a new miner and send her in that condition into the mine—a rite that had long been abandoned.

Sexual harassment was endemic. In oral histories compiled by Marat Moore, the former associate editor of the *United Mineworkers Journal*, women describe a variety of indignities they suffered in the mines: groping, sexual jokes, physical assaults, displays of pornography throughout the mines, and other problems like finding human feces in a dinner bucket.[23] As one miner explained, "They're just going to sexually abuse us until we drop out of the competition. I've been told I can make more money lying on my back at the pit mouth than working back in the mine."[24] Patricia Brown shared her early experience in the coal mines:

I have a big bust. I never thought about it until I got down there. They made me feel ashamed. They would tease and comment and write things on the walls. They drew pictures. Some guy on the shift before me would go down and draw pictures of my body, and somebody else would come and tell me, so everybody would get a big laugh ... The first time I saw it, I went home and cried.[25]

The women did not find refuge in their unions.

In the late 1970s, women miners at the unionized Consolidation Coal Company discovered a pencil-sized hole drilled into a wall in their shower area. They became suspicious after very specific graffiti appeared in the mine, "such as calling so and so 'scar back' (the woman had had a back operation) and saying so and so had 'inverted nipples.'"[26] When they complained, the men accused the women of knowing about the peephole and openly parading in front of it to turn them on. The women filed a grievance with their union, the United Mine Workers of America (UMWA), but the union refused to process the grievance because the contract did not have privacy language. The women sued the company for more than $5 million and settled during a dramatic trial that "took on many aspects of a rape trial."[27] Union men and the local union mine committee chairman testified on behalf of the company, attacking the women's credibility.

Lois Jenson, one of the first women to work in the iron ore mines of northern Minnesota, suffered a similar experience. Her painful and heroic story was fictionalized in the motion picture *North Country*. Women were met with hostility and vituperation from the men in the Eveleth mine, who forcefully protected the mine's "distinctly macho worldview."[28] As Lois Jenson began work on her second day on the job, a male coworker walked past her and, without looking at her or breaking his stride, said, "You fucking women don't belong here. If you knew what was good for you, you'd go home where you belong."[29] The vitriol never dissipated.

In court, the women testified to what they had endured in their work lives: being groped, grabbed, pressured for sex, threatened with rape, and subjected to pornography and crass graffiti throughout the plant, and constant graphic conversations about sex. One woman testified that on three separate occasions, she found "a gob of fresh semen" on clothes that she kept in her locker.[30] Three years after the case was filed, a sign appeared and remained in the break-room bulletin board that read in all capital letters, "sexual harassment in this area will not be reported. However, it will be graded."[31]

Violence in the plant intensified as women pressed their complaints. Women testified that they were stalked at home and began carrying weapons to defend themselves against physical attacks. A young man testified to "watching his mother pack her lunch box for work each day: a knife, mace, rope to tie shut the door to her work area, and food."[32]

The women were members of United Steelworkers (USW) Local 6860, yet the union provided them no sanctuary or support. When Lois Jenson turned to the union after years of being stalked and physically threatened by a supervisor, the union steward told her that he did not know how to file a sexual harassment grievance, even though he had been trained on how to file such grievances. Another woman described in court that she was repeatedly exposed to graffiti about men who said they "sucked her cunt and her juicy red lips," and when she complained about the graffiti to the union president, he shrugged and said, "Well, it's true, isn't it?"[33]

The women knew that they should only complain about the conduct of supervisors, not their male coworkers or the union, because "to be a squealer was to betray the entire union movement, tantamount to becoming a company spy," a sentiment that remains too common among women unionists today. Yet, their complaints only pushed the union to side more closely with the company against them.

Union officials made no secret of their views about the women's claims and which members deserved protection from the union. The union president testified: "It's my job to represent the employees and the members of my union out there … and it's not my job to give discipline. It's my job to protect them from discipline."[34]

Many women miners who were brutalized didn't even attempt to file grievances because they knew that they would not be addressed. Patsey Farley was among the first women to work at one of the largest coal mines in eastern Kentucky in the late 1970s. As Marat Moore explains, "She survived more than most people could endure: a troubled childhood, domestic abuse, the loss of her children in a custody battle, job harassment, unemployment, and battles with her employer and with her union."[35] Farley exposed sexual harassment and discrimination and blew the whistle on company payoffs to the government agency that oversees safety at the mines, the Mine Safety and Health Administration (MSHA). She and her female coworkers did this alone. As she explained, "The union wouldn't help us. If a man complained, they'd take care of it. With the women, it was, 'Bless their little stupid hearts. Wonder what they're quarreling about now.'"[36] Patricia Brown, the coal miner who found drawings of her body in the mine, "never went to the union about it because then the company brands you a troublemaker. If I had gone to them with a discrimination grievance, it would have meant more discrimination."[37]

As one miner's lawyer explained, after the boss repeatedly told her client to "put out or get out," "the union took the position that this issue is not something it's going to fight for. When the union says it's helping women, it just doesn't wash. The women are on their own."[38] And worse, if they complained, they regularly faced brutal retaliation.

When Darla Baker started working at the Consolidated Coal Company, the personnel manager told her that she should expect to be "grabbed by the ass and boobs" and that there was nothing he could do to stop it. What she suffered was far worse. A coworker tried to rape her underground. She escaped to an underground lunchroom, where a supervisor and eight miners took a lunch break. The attacker followed her there and attacked her again while the others looked on and laughed. She reported the incident to management and the union, but nothing happened to her attacker. Her work life, on the other hand, became hell. She found her tires slashed, and rumors spread that she had a bed hidden in the mine where she worked as a prostitute. The men wrote her new nickname, "Deep Throat Darla, the blow job miner," in chalk all over the mine. Women at the mine who suffered similar experiences reported that comments and indignities

are not isolated events happening once a week or month, but something we have to live with every single day we work. We've complained to the personnel manager, but he just laughs, and so do the local United Mine Workers' Union leaders. It is a condition of our jobs, and no matter what we try, it never goes away.[39]

In construction, tradeswomen fought their way into the industry and suffered rampant sex discrimination in the industry and sex discrimination in hiring and at work. They "were met with universal hostility, contempt, or passive disregard" and faced vicious hazing, sexual harassment, and isolation.[40] Men sexualized every aspect of the job, from tools to basic tasks. Nancy Quick's poem "Construction Lango" captures the culture that tradeswomen endured in the 1970s:

Do you know how to screw?
How deep is your hole?
Is that rod coming thru?
Nail that piece, baby!
Put it in there girl!!!
May I have a nut or two?
Construction lango …
That's what I call it,
We hear it every day.[41]

Like in the mines, sexual harassment was a tool that men used to show women their place and punish them for invading male spheres of power. When women entered the construction division of Local 3 of the International Brotherhood of Electrical Workers (IBEW)—one of the most powerful unions in the country whose members were regarded as "the aristocracy of labor,"[42] given their high wages, shorter working days, and generous benefits—they met a hostile reception. "Their presence did not square with the men's perceptions of women who were wives, daughters, mothers, lovers, and whores—not future electricians."[43]

The industry and the union did little to prepare the basics for women entering the trades. Bathrooms and changing facilities were scarce—and in many construction sites still are. Pornography was rampant. The women understood that men used pornography to make a point: "'You're not welcome here. You're in our territory.' You walk in the locker [room], and the guys start reading out loud from a porno magazine." The union refused to do anything about it. When a group of apprentices wrote to Thomas Van Arsdale, Local 3 Business Manager, he told them that "it is a personal matter for the membership" and that he "can't interfere with the personal lives of the membership."[44] Van Arsdale later testified to the New City Commission on Human Rights in 1993:

It's hard to say that some woman was unable to maintain a job because she complained about photographs or some individual relieving himself in full view, which has been traditional in New York City. I don't think it's fair to describe that as sexual harassment. I don't think it endangers the individual's chances of being a success on the job. I would say pornography is common in our industry.[45]

Women endured much more than pornography. When Linda Jokfu was an apprentice electrician, while installing a doorbell and working with live wires, three male coworkers dumped a bucket of water on her. "They really just wanted to see my wet T-shirt," she told a journalist. "That's the kind of antics you dealt with on a daily basis. You really feel like quitting." Later, when she was installing a garbage disposal on her back, with her head and hands under the sink, a coworker attempted to fondle her: she felt the handle of a hammer and a coworker's hands groping between her legs. She quit a few weeks later, remarking, "It's very difficult to fight for yourself when you're isolated, when you're the only woman. You feel there's something wrong with you."[46]

Black women faced the intersecting harms of sexism and vile racism. The historian Jean Schroeder collected the oral histories of women who entered blue-collar jobs in the 1970s and 1980s. She captured the voices of union women like electrician Anna Brinkley, who explained, "Being racist and sexist is one of the unwritten rules of social acceptance in the trades."[47] Ms. Brinkley shared:

There was one woman who worked in the production area that I got along well with until she saw my children in the parking lot one day. Then she started a whole series of racist jokes every time I had to come into her area. It turned out that she was a member of a Klan organization and was a real redneck. The guys in the shop really liked her. She made it difficult to establish standards with the guys, because she used to hang *Playboy* pictures and, worse, *Hustler* pictures all over the walls. Anyhow, when her comments failed to irritate me, she left a supposed-joke thing called "Nigger's Application for Employment" in my tool box. You ever seen it? It's the worst piece of racist shit I've ever seen. It had, like, "What kind of things do you prefer to eat?" And then all the cliche type of soul food things, "What kind of car do you prefer—Lincoln Continental, Cadillac … ?" "What's your favorite pastime—screwing white women?" It was just really gross, so I took it to my superintendent, and he said, "Well, what's wrong with this? This has been going around for years. What do you want me to do with this?"

Building trades unions were in denial about the harassment. According to a 1991 *Los Angeles Times* report, at a meeting of

Women at Work, a support group for women in the trades, every hand in the room shot up when an organizer asked the three dozen or so women present how many had been sexually harassed on the job. "It's 100% prevalent," she told the *Times*. Yet, men in the trades denied a problem existed.[48]

John Scott, director of an electrical apprenticeship program in San Francisco, said, "We anticipated problems on the job site with harassment, but just the opposite turned out … The men pamper them, treat them like daughters. They're too easy on them." Calvin Emery, the business manager of the Plumbers Union Local 78 in Los Angeles, told the *Los Angeles Times* that "all the old stuff you may have heard about years ago doesn't happen anymore." "The women are making a good showing; they're well accepted," added an officer of the Operating Engineers Union, Local 3.

Women who sought skilled craft jobs in the telecommunications industry didn't fare much better. Women obtained those jobs not through the advocacy of their unions but through litigation by the EEOC. As Jane LaTour recounts, the Communications Workers of America (CWA) played no active role in the EEOC's efforts, including participating in discussions over the terms of a court-monitored settlement agreement. The union, however, later sued to stop implementation of the settlement agreement because it overrode seniority. As Ilene Winkler, one of the first women to serve as a switching equipment technician and a member of CWA Local 1101, explained, "I found out that there had never really been a seniority system for promotions in the first place. So it felt to us like they had gone to court to keep women out of the job."[49]

Women who entered the skilled crafts in the phone company were also met with vicious sexual harassment. Venus Green describes one such incident:

One time, for this young woman's birthday, they gave her a party and brought a big birthday cake and put a dildo in it. Women who would not let them touch them were marked, either as gay or [as] a problem ... So once you have an attitude problem, then you get put into the ugly bin. You know? "She's just ugly." Sometimes the racism [and sexism] would be so explicit. Like, for example, if some woman from another part of the company came down on the floor for whatever reason, with high heels and a dress, they would carry on about, "Oh, it's so wonderful to have something beautiful come in here, given what we have to see every day" ... That kind of comment.[50]

Winkler and her union sisters set up a Women's Committee within the Local, but when the women attempted to take up the issue of extreme sexual harassment faced by the women in the craft jobs, the Local disbanded the committee. The women were left to fight harassment by themselves through lawsuits that were settled with secrecy clauses that essentially silenced the women and allowed the systemic harassment to continue.[51]

Women in the auto plants fared no better. As their numbers grew in the industry during the 1970s, they confronted a masculine shop culture that was "coarser, grosser, and more violent" than the sexist culture of earlier years. In the past, supervisors had been the primary harassers and abusers, but now coworkers became the harassers.[52] Women "endured the inappropriate language and touching and the degrading and humiliating treatment their workmates meted out. At the same time, the shop floor was a man's world, and upper-level managers, local union officials, and arbitrators were indifferent to the plight of women."[53]

In the mid-1990s, the EEOC sued Mitsubishi Motors on behalf of a group of United Auto Workers (UAW) women who were tormented by sexual harassment for years. That lawsuit was one of the largest sexual harassment cases in the nation's history. Hundreds of women complained of abusive behavior for years. In that case, the EEOC investigation found obscene, crude sketches of genital organs and sex acts and names of female workers scratched into unpainted car bodies moving along the assembly line. Women were called sluts, whores, and bitches, and subjected to groping, forced sex play, and male flashing. Explicit sexual graffiti such as "KILL THE SLUT MARY" were scrawled on the rest area and bathroom walls.[54]

Men also assaulted women with factory equipment, placing hoses, wrenches, and air guns between women's legs. They also sabotaged women's work and posted lists on the walls, ranking the women in the plant by their estimated breast sizes.

The union did nothing. Terry Paz reported to the union that a coworker "grabbed her breasts, wiggled his tongue at her, and asked what sex positions she liked best."[55] She also complained that the coworker would follow her around her neighborhood and was writing graffiti about her in the men's room of a local bar. She repeatedly tried to get the union to file a grievance based on a hostile work environment, but the union refused. Later, when she complained directly to the company and the harasser was fired, the union stepped in on his behalf to challenge the discipline.

Other women complained that photographs of sex parties were being passed around in the workplace; the union did nothing about those complaints.

The lawsuit settled for $34 million, which was distributed among 400 women and amounted to the largest sexual harassment settlement as of the late 1990s. The settlement also required the company to adopt an anti-sexual harassment policy and create a three-person panel of outside monitors to ensure that the policy is implemented. The union was not on that panel.

Male unionists didn't always abandon their sisters: in 1979, 1400 male lumber workers, members of Local 3-38 of the International Woodworkers of America (IWA), shut down three logging camps and five mills in Shelton, Washington, in support of a female member of the union fired for refusing to drop her charges of sexual harassment against the Simpson Lumber Company. The woman, along with six of her union sisters, signed affidavits reporting that during their hiring interviews, they had been "asked to take off their blouses and endure comments about their breasts." The union president told the press, "As male chauvinistic as our workers might be, even they don't tolerate that kind of interview process."[56]

WOMEN FIGHT BACK

Despite the persistent and systemic efforts by male trade unionists to marginalize and isolate them, women fought back against sexual harassment and abuse collectively and individually in a variety of ways.

In 1912, about 800 corset makers and members of the International Ladies Garment Workers' Union (ILGWU) went on strike in Kalamazoo, Michigan. At first, the women sought an increase in pay and union recognition, but sexual harassment soon surfaced as the major strike issue. Workers complained that the foremen awarded the better jobs to women who slept with them. One woman complained, "The management of that concern is run by superintendents, some of them diseased and

29

filthy, whose minds are occupied more with carnal pleasure than with the business of the firm."[57]

Similarly, women button makers, members of Button Workers' Protective Union 12845 in Iowa, went on strike in 1911. There, too, sexual harassment was a major issue. The women insisted that the managers used their power to force sexual relations on the women. One manager, for example, maintained a "resting room" where women who gave "in to his devilish demands were reciprocated with a steady job. Those who did not comply with his wishes received discharge notices."[58]

Individually, as they have done through the ages, women figured out how to manage on the job site. Wendy, an apprentice heavy equipment operator, told a women's trades publication, "I'm feeling that I'm always the one that has to be nice, to soothe the men's egos, and not offend them. And I've also found that it's not stopping them. I'm wondering: maybe I should get nasty." That didn't work, either.[59] Paulette, an apprentice in the Electrician's Union, said that she tried to use humor: "Jesus, you sound like a bunch of jackasses," and that held them off a little while. "In the summertime, when it was hot and I had nothing but a T-shirt on, a guy said to me, 'Well, we can't all bounce like you,'" so she started to wear a bra again, though she hadn't worn one in years.[60] Pat, a journey-level union carpenter summarized her strategy:

I think it's real important that women do not feel power-less individually, that they learn to assert themselves. I think also being direct, dealing with stuff directly—especially sexual harassment—instead of just trying to ignore it and moving away. I think women need to use their individual power and not feel that they always have to rely on government and superintendents.[61]

Women also formed organizations that created spaces where they could strategize and share their experiences of entering male-dominated work. In 1977, mining women organized the Coal Employment Project (CEP), a grassroots organization that served as a hub for leadership development, legal activism, and moral and emotional support.[62] CEP hosted annual conferences that became a forum for union women to share views on a variety of issues including reproductive rights, the Equal Rights Amendment and sexual harassment. At the first National Conference of Women Coal Miners in June 1979, sexual harassment was only mentioned "in whispers, in corners here and there."[63] Initially, "women were too embarrassed, ashamed and isolated to report sexual harassment, feeling that they had somehow provoked the behavior." Once women started sharing their experiences, the tide turned. Sexual harassment emerged as a major theme of the second National Conference of Women Coal Miners in 1980. Workshops on the subject were packed, and one woman exclaimed, "At last! Somebody else has been going through all this! I thought it was just me!" The CEP surveyed women on their experiences of harassment and published guidelines for legal and contractual remedies. In 1981, CEP published the results of the survey, which showed rampant and violent sexual harassment of women coal miners: 54 percent of women were propositioned by the bosses, 76 percent were propositioned by coworkers and 17 percent had been attacked physically.[64]

Tradeswomen established Tradeswomen, Inc. (TWI) in 1979, which was one of the first organizations for women in the trades. It continues to be one of the most active and effective organizations in the nation focused exclusively on the needs of women in the skilled trades. Its mission is to recruit more women into the trades and develop the capacity for leadership on the job and in their unions. TWI published *Tradeswomen* magazine, the only national magazine written by and for women in the trades. Today, there are more than twelve local organizations for women in trades, helping women build skills, network, connect to unions, and learn to fight against harassment and abuse.

Women also found accountability through the courts, in large part without their unions by their side. To the contrary, unions stood as defendants or bystanders in the early cases that set the boundaries of what constitutes "hostile work environment" sexual harassment, and how the law addresses that form of workplace discrimination.[65] For example, the groundbreaking case that established the "reasonable woman" standard, upon which hostile work environment claims are evaluated, *Ellison v. Brady*, was brought by a woman who was employed at the Internal Revenue Service and a member of the National Treasury Employees Union. Lois Robinson, a welder and union member, successfully sued her employer, Jacksonville Shipyards, securing for the first time legal recognition of the role that pornography plays in creating a hostile environment in violation of the Civil Rights Act. In all of these cases, the women's unions played no positive roles in their struggles, or in their legal victories.

If the court cases tell us anything, it is that unions' attitudes about sexual harassment of their members—especially by their male members—have not changed all that much. In August 2017, the EEOC reached a $10 million settlement with Ford over racial and sexual harassment allegations at the very same Chicago plants.[66] The union played no positive role. To the contrary, that year, at least one woman accused the UAW bargaining committee chairman, Allen "Coby" Millender, of repeated assaults that included touching, grabbing, and attempts at unwanted kissing. When one woman sought his help after being fired, he told her she would have to get on her knees and "act like another woman who moments before their conversation, had been pressed close to him, standing between his legs."[67]

Save for the failed efforts of one steward, the union took no steps to protect the women, yet went out of its way to protect the accused harasser. When Millender received a two-week suspension following a company investigation, the union complained on his behalf and took his case to arbitration. When plant rumors spread that Millender had been fired, UAW vice president Jimmy Settles quickly took to Facebook to clarify that Millender had not been fired, only suspended, and noted that "the UAW has filed a grievance challenging Mr. Millender's suspension."[68] By contrast, the union made no statement concerning the brutal conditions that its female members were forced to endure at the hands of supervisors and union agents.

Understanding this history is essential in crafting a new way forward. Assumptions about the role of women, and tolerance for misogyny disguised as "horseplay" or "boys will be boys" are still alive within many union cultures. Those elements must be rooted out, with intention. As we shall see in the following chapters, some unions have made positive steps in that direction.

2

Unions Under the #MeToo Spotlight

What's a Monet? It's like a painting, see? From far away, it's OK, but up close, it's a big old mess.

—Cher Horowitz[1]

#MeToo did not come as a surprise to working women; we had been waiting for a reckoning for decades, if not centuries. The hashtag originated in 2006 when Tarana Burke launched a campaign to raise awareness about the prevalence of sexual harassment and sexual assault, especially in marginalized communities. It caught fire in 2017 when exposés of the now convicted rapist and former Holywood mogul Harvey Weinstein prompted an outpouring of similar stories from millions of survivors around the world. Nonetheless, it caught unions flat-footed.

Labor-friendly commentators and the AFL-CIO responded by promoting unionization as the answer. "We are not going to solve the problem unless we address the profoundly undemocratic structure of most workplaces," said one commentator, adding "a union grievance procedure at least gives workers an opportunity to appeal to a neutral decision maker."[2] The AFL-CIO published an article on its website that argued, "[g]iven that sexual harassment is an abuse of power, typically by a male manager against female subordinates, having a union and collective voice strengthens a worker's ability to stop harassment. A woman facing sexual harassment is not alone."[3]

There's nothing necessarily wrong with these ideas: workers *do* need unions, and workplaces *are* undemocratic. One problem is that those arguments are based on two flawed assumptions: (1) that victims of sexual harassment have access to union grievance procedures in all—or at least, most—unionized workplaces, and (2) that harassers are, in most instances, the boss.

To the contrary, research shows that 60 percent of women who experience harassment on the job are harrassed by their peers, while only 28 percent report harassment by a manager or supervisor.[4] And, as we'll explore further, unions have a poor track record of using grievance mechanisms or their power in the shop in favor of women who are harassed at work, especially if the harasser is a coworker.

A bigger problem is that these responses ignore the union's own role in the problem. Professor Marion Crain, who studied all reported legal cases and arbitral opinions involving unions and sexual harassment between 1970 and 1995, concluded that

> most unions contribute to women's economic disempower-ment by addressing sexual harassment in a manner that discourages women from acting collectively through their unions to combat such treatment in the workplace. This casts the union as simply another level of patriarchy for women unionists to contend with in the workplace, rather than as an ally.[5]

The labor movement did not exactly lead the charge in the #MeToo phenomenon. On a positive note, women members of the Animation Guild, IATSE Local 839 took a creative approach to holding accountable one of the first men to fall in the wake of #MeToo, Chris Savino, a Nickelodeon showrunner and the creator of the popular show *The Loud House*.[6] The studio fired Savino within a few weeks of the Harvey Weinstein revelations after multiple women came forward with sexual harassment allegations.[7] After his firing, a growing number of women shared stories in a private Facebook group of how Savino had "leveraged his power to ensure they went along with his lewd suggestions and come-ons."[8] Savino posted an apology on Facebook, which did not sit well with at least one of the women. "I think 'I'm sorry' is not enough," she said.[9] The women filed charges with their union alleging that Savino violated a provision in the union's bylaws that punishes "disloyalty," including "disloyalty to this Local, and/or disloyalty to fellow members."[10]

A day before the trial was set to start, Savino agreed to a one-year suspension, 40 hours of community service, sexual harassment training, and therapy, along with the distribution of a letter to all union signatory studios informing them of Savino's suspension.[11] He was not permitted to work for any union signatory studio during his suspension. Some women wanted him out of the union, but the settlement turned out to be the best possible outcome. Because of arcane union rules, if the union expelled Savino, a union shop could still hire him, and the union would have to pay his dues.[12]

While the animators were using the power of their union to hold a harasser accountable, the most prominent unions and the AFL-CIO were too busy dealing with their own scandals and other problematic behavior.

The spotlight initially fell on the Screen Actors Guild–Federation of Television and Radio Artists (SAG-AFTRA), which is not surprising, given the entertainment industry's high level of unionization, the fact that the union already had a "zero tolerance" policy on sexual harassment, and, well, Harvey Weinstein. Journalists asked the hard questions: "Why did none of the women whom Weinstein harassed or assaulted feel like they could go to their union for help? How could he hurt so many people for so long and still remain at the top of his field? What did the union know about Harvey Weinstein, and when did it know it?"[13]

SAG-AFTRA members were unhappy. Meissa Hampton, an actress and founder of the Actors Alliance for Gender Equity in Media, published an op-ed in the *Guardian*, where she outlined her efforts to secure the union's attention to the issue of sexual harassment in 2015.[14] The actress authored a petition asking the union "to address gender inequities that fuel the culture of sexual abuse in the industry," and suggesting an internal committee to tackle issues of discrimination. Her efforts failed. Similarly, the actress Mia Kirshner penned an op-ed for the Toronto *Globe and Mail* titled "I was not protected from Harvey Weinstein. It's time for institutional change".[15] Speaking directly to her union, she cautioned that "change does not mean publishing another well-meaning brochure or email blast about anti-harassment policies. Statements pledging support for survivors of sexual harassment and assault are not going to cut it."[16]

While the union eventually articulated a long-term, inclusive approach rooted in cultural change to eradicate sexual harassment, the union's initial response was much more cautious, focusing on the union's own liability. David White, SAG's then-national executive director, explained in an email to a SAG board member, "This is one of those extremely big, emotionally sensitive, legally complex issues that has serious legal implications for SAG-AFTRA, as well as several of our members, who may look to us for protection as this process unfolds."[17] White also noted in that email that the union's lawyers "are very involved to ensure we don't have any missteps that bring on liability in any way."[18]

The union had been involved in high-profile cases of accusations of sexual harassment by its members in recent years, which puts this cautious response in context. In 2015, for example, the union publicly battled the documentarian Amy Berg in relation to her film about sexual abuse of child actors in Hollywood.[19] The documentary, *An Open Secret*, included an interview conducted at the union's offices with Michael Harrah, a former child actor, cofounder and former chair of the union's Young Performers Committee. The interview revealed Harrah's questionable relationships with child actors; Harrah resigned from the SAG-AFTRA Committee a few days after the interview.

The feud between the union and producers involved references in the film to SAG-AFTRA, which the union demanded be removed from the film entirely, and the producers refused. While the documentary did not blame the union for the abuse, the documentarian repeatedly asked the union what it planned to do about the troubling allegations the film uncovered. The union told Berg that it is not a law enforcement organization, does not have the power to investigate crimes, and referred the producer to law enforcement.[20]

In January 2018, the union honored the actor Morgan Freeman with a Lifetime Achievement Award. Four months later, CNN reported a pattern of sexually harassing behavior by the actor.[21] His alleged conduct included repeatedly attempting to lift a production assistant's skirt, and telling a reporter who was pregnant at the time, "you are ripe," after he shook her hand, looked her up and down, and said, "I wish I was there."[22]

The union issued a statement that said, "These are compelling and devastating allegations which are absolutely contrary to all the steps that we are taking to (ensure) a safe work environment for the professionals in this industry."[23] Further, "given Mr. Freeman recently received one of our union's most prestigious honors recognizing his body of work, we are therefore reviewing what corrective actions may be warranted at this time." As it turns out, the answer is none.[24]

SAG-AFTRA has taken steps in the right direction. It adopted an initiative, "The Four Pillars of Change," whose mission is to identify "real solutions and actions that help members confront harassment while securing an equitable workplace."[25]

The initiative includes a new code of conduct that focuses heavily on the employer's responsibility vis-à-vis sexual harassment: "Employers have a legal and contractual obligation to maintain a workplace free from sexual harassment. SAG-AFTRA is committed to holding employers accountable for this obligation."[26] In reference to the union's own responsibilities, it simply lays out the steps that the union will take if a member chooses to complete a complaint questionnaire. Deflecting full responsibility to the employer for preventing and addressing sexual harassment is not uncommon among unions.

Some positive steps have emerged from SAG-AFTRA's efforts, including the end of work-related meetings being held in hotel rooms. Yet, reports of how the union is enforcing the code of conduct leaves room for pause. In 2018, the actress Sarah Scott filed a complaint against fellow actor Kip Perdue after he masturbated in front of her shortly before filming a scene with her, and then placed her hand on his crotch as they lay under the covers while waiting to film the scene. A year later, a SAG-AFTRA disciplinary committee held the actor guilty of "serious misconduct" and fined him $6000, with the option of reducing that already paltry fine by half if he took an online sexual harassment course.[27] The union has now established protocols for on-set nudity and created a registry of accredited intimacy coordinators.[28]

Unions' responses to #MeToo were also crippled by their own internal scandals.

The AFL-CIO's chief budget officer, Terry Stapleton, resigned in shame in November 2017 as Bloomberg prepared a story that he'd sent lewd text messages to a secretary and for pressing her to come to this hotel room."[29] Scott Courtney, Service Employees International Union (SEIU) executive vice president and the architect of the Fight for $15 campaign, resigned in October of that year, while the union's general counsel was investigating him for years of inappropriate behavior, including "sexual misconduct and abusive behavior."[30] Buzzfeed reported that "the complaints about Courtney had been an open secret among women in the high-profile Fight for $15 campaign within the union, which is itself led by one of the most visible women in the U.S. labor movement."[31] Courtney married a young union staffer while on suspension the weekend before he resigned.[32]

Kendall Fells and Caleb Jennings, two other top leaders in the Fight for $15 high-profile campaign also stepped down in October of that year while being investigated for abusive behavior directed mostly at women.[33]

The most troubling example of behavior that, if it existed in any non-union workplace, would have union leaders up in arms involves David Regan, the president of SEIU's largest local union, United Healthcare Workers West (UHW), in California. In 2018, Mindy Sturge, a former UHW staff person, alleged in court filings that she was drugged and sexually assaulted by a senior union staffer.[34] Ms. Sturge submitted sworn declarations that reveal a culture of misogyny, abuse of power, entitlement, and abuse:[35]

- "Early on in my employment, I was told by my supervisor that instead of complaining about workplace issues, I should 'put my big girl panties on.' I was also told that if I wanted to get ahead at UHW, I should hang out and drink with President Dave Regan and the upper management around him."

- "At a multi-day union event in Portland in August 2017, I was standing near Mr. Regan in a room where women from other unions were dancing. He told me I should get out on the dance floor because all the 'fat ass' nurses were dancing. He also referred to them as 'fat bitches.' It was not the first time I had heard him use that term to refer to someone—he used it once in his office (where other managers were present) to refer to the wife of one of the employers with whom we deal."

- "[Dave Regan] also made a comment to me, 'Does the carpet match the drapes.' I learned that it was a reference to the color of my pubic hair, and it made me very uncomfortable."

- "I personally observed Mr. Regan staring at former Political Director [redacted] at union events. I have also seen him on the dance floor grinding against women union members or staff in an inappropriate manner, and he has done this with me, too. It was embarrassing."

- "Mr. Regan screamed profanity at me in public for talking with him about sexual harassment issues."

- "At one Eboard event, I saw Dave Regan standing with Division Director Chokri Bensaid. A woman member

41

from Kaiser passed by (her name was [redacted]) and Dave Regan said, 'The only way she is getting a job [with UHW] is if she sucks my dick.' Later, I learned that the woman was given a staff job with UHW. I found Mr. Regan's behavior to be very inappropriate."

- "I was sent to Arizona for about two weeks ... While there, I was asked to drive Dave Regan and UHW Vice President Stan Lyles to 'the nearest watering hole' (bar). While the three of us were in the car together, Dave Regan said 'hopefully I can pick up some 'ho's' because all the 'ho's' in the Arizona office are ugly."

- "It is my experience from being on Eboard that if you do not agree with everything Dave Regan wants to do, you will be shunned or the union will try to find a way to retaliate against you. I have personally seen this happen to people on Eboard."

- "Mr. Regan is a notorious 'boob gazer', meaning he would stare at women's breasts. One member, [redacted], told me that she had to tell Mr. Regan, 'Dave, my eyes are up here' when he would be staring at her breasts."

In January, 2020, on the eve of trial, the union settled the lawsuit for an undisclosed amount. The terms of the settlement include a Nondisclosure Agreement (NDA), which bars the survivor from discussing any aspects of her story.[36]

In the course of her lawsuit, Ms. Sturge wrote to the International Union asking for help changing the work environment. She explained that "staff members are afraid to speak out, and prior complaints about some of the men who created this hostile environment have gone nowhere."[37] She closed the letter as follows: "I love this union and I want it to become a better workplace for everyone."

She received a response from the International's General Counsel two weeks later, thanking her for sharing her concerns, but refusing to provide any assistance as "the International Union does not have a direct role in investigating allegations or concerns that arise in local unions regarding personnel matters."[38]

Regan remains president of the local, a vice president of the International, and sits on the executive board of the International.[39]

The International appointed an external advisory board to look into sexual misconduct, which included high-profile women: Cecilia Muñoz, formerly in the Obama Administration, Debra Katz, who represented Dr. Christine Blasey Ford during the Supreme Court nomination hearing of Justice Brett Kavanaugh, and Fatima Goss Graves, president of the National Women's law center.[40] The union hasn't released any information about the work of this advisory board, and there is nothing in the public record other than its formation.

There are signs that some unions are moving towards a new paradigm. We'll explore those in these pages, especially SEIU United Service Workers West (USWW), which is the gold standard in addressing sexual harassment. The complexity and contradictions that surround unions' handling of sexual harassment are particularly clear when it comes to SEIU. Paradoxically, within the state of California, two of its largest locals co-exist. One is led by Latinas who are creatively crafting a new path forward, and the other is headed by Dave Regan. This paradox underscores the need for systemic change and accountability throughout the labor movement.

3
The Survivors

They tried to bury us; they didn't know we were seeds
—Mexican proverb cribbed from
the Greek poet Dino Christianopoulos

Four people deeply dedicated to the labor movement shared their experiences dealing with sexual harassment on the job and the role that their unions played in their traumatic stories. These are stories of resilience, strength, anger, and pain—not victim porn. These resilient and committed human beings embody what this writer believes is the essence of what the labor movement needs to grow and thrive.

SARA WILDER

Sara grew up in Meriden, Kansas, a small, picturesque town nestled in the rolling plains of the Midwestern United States. Sara could have been a character in the classic 1984 film *Footloose*. Sara was raised in a strict Christian home, the middle child of seven; she was not allowed to wear pants, go to dances, or play cards.[1] She was a country girl and a "girlie tomboy." She ran around her family's farm and played with Barbies, trucks, G.I. Joes, and cows.

She gave birth to a baby boy just after finishing high school and married her high school sweetheart. Sara had another baby a year later, and her husband went into the military and off to fight in Desert Storm. Having just turned 19, Sara found herself living alone near a remote military base in Kansas, with two babies, and having to teach herself how to drive a stick shift. It is an endearing testament to her sweet yet tough disposition that she equates single motherhood with driving a stick shift.

Her first marriage didn't last very long. However, a few years later, she married the love of her life, and they raised five children. They've been together for 27 years.

Sara started her work at the Goodyear Tire and Rubber plant in Topeka, Kansas, nearly 20 years ago. Sara drove a forklift in the warehouse for the first three years and then moved to processing as a mill operator. She was responsible for operating machinery used to layer rubber sheets with other materials to create the structure of a tire. One of her proudest accomplishments is that she is one of the few people in the world to make tires for the U.S. President's limousine. She was part of a secret process where she ran the machine that made eight tires for President Obama's limousine alone in the room with her supervisor.

The rubber plant was represented by Local 307 of the United Steelworkers. She became involved with the union as soon as she walked in the door and in its United Way fundraising campaign, which the union strongly supported. The charity and the employer have an agreement that allows the charity to collect funds directly from union members—with the members' approval—during an annual fundraising drive known as "the campaign." Sara, along with other union volunteers, spent part of the year encouraging fellow union members to volunteer and contribute to the charity's efforts.

In 2014, a staff position opened at the United Way, and Sara jumped at the chance. As a "labor liaison" at the United Way, Sara would broaden the universe from which she could raise money for the charity, bringing in unions that until then had never contributed to the United Way.

The liaison's job is to participate in fundraising events, which bring together leaders, staff, and members of the various local unions that contribute to the United Way. A couple of years into her job, Sara attended an event at a local bar where the charity's staff and volunteers, functioning as servers, were dressed in costumes. One volunteer was dressed as Dolly Parton, the country music icon known for embracing her curves and accentuating her femininity with glittering sequins and flashy rhinestones. During this event, a man who represented the steelworkers on the board of the United Way offered the server donned as Dolly Parton five dollars to "motorboat" him, that is, to put his face between her breasts and blow. Sara was floored but not surprised.

This man, who we'll call Mike, had been groping and propositioning Sara for years. At an event in 2016, he told Sara, as he put his hands between her legs, "You know, given the opportunity to fuck you, I'd do it in a heartbeat." He was drunk; people laughed. Sara felt humiliated.

Sara had reported Mike to her union president several times. Her union's president dismissed her each time. Once, he told her, "You wanted to be in a union. This is what it's like."[2] He later told her, "He's my best buddy; what do you expect me to do?" Although she had decided that complaining was futile, she stepped forward in 2016 after she attended a conference that addressed the topic of sexual harassment, which I describe in the Introduction.

Like so many women before her, the institutions failed Sara. She filed a complaint with the United Way, her employer's Human Resources Department, and asked the HR representative to keep it confidential. Shortly after that, Sara started receiving text messages saying things like, "You cunt, how dare you go after Mike?" The HR representative had told Mike about Sara's complaint because, as she told Sara, "he had a right to know."

Things got worse for Sara. Instead of supporting her and making sure that Sara was safe, the union intervened on Mike's behalf. The union sent a representative, Mark, to tell the United Way they wanted Sara "off the campaign," meaning she would no longer work on fundraising drives at unionized companies. Mark was at the bar in 2016 when Mike propositioned Sara. United Way obliged and assigned Sara to work on other non-union fundraising drives, but the betrayal stung. She felt betrayed, alone, and marginalized.

Everywhere Sara turned within her union world, she ran into roadblocks. She tried to get help from the local arm of the AFL-CIO, filing a complaint for retaliation, but the federation told her they were not interested in pursuing the charge. Sara then wrote to Richard Trumka, the national AFL-CIO president, asking him to investigate. She received a curt response saying they'd get back to her, but she never heard back.

Her efforts to get help from her union's headquarters were equally futile. Sara spoke with a lawyer for the national United Steelworkers, who refused to address Sara's concerns and told her that the union could do nothing because everything she relayed was "not a union function." Sara understood that her union did not believe sexual harassment was a union issue.

Nor did Sara get any help from the Women of Steel, which self-describes as "an activist arm of the USW that evolved from the early women's caucuses that demanded that women have their rightful place in the union."[3] The first time she reported harassment to them, she was told, "There was absolutely nothing that they could help me with about that." In

2018, when the group sent a mass email with a reminder that the union "was a zero-tolerance organization," she hit the reply-all button (to over 300 women) with several rolling eyes emojis noting that "the email was an absolute joke!" She told them that they "all knew harassment was going on and chose to sweep it under the rug." She was immediately blocked from the listserv but received emails from other women saying they appreciated her speaking up because that was their experience.

Sara left the United Way in 2019 and returned to the rubber tire plant. She felt she had no choice. As she told me, she "just wanted it to stop. Everyone saw what Mike was doing, and no one had my back."

Sara is happy back at the plant, even though she didn't feel welcomed by her union siblings. She earned a $10,000 raise when she returned. Her benefits are excellent, and her schedule lets her spend lots of time with her grandbabies. Before the harassment started, Sara never missed a union meeting. During the five dark years she was dealing with harassment, she didn't attend a single meeting. Sara recently told the vice president of her union about everything that happened to her. She finally found an empathetic ear. "He was so saddened to hear it and begged me to start getting involved again." She's slowly making her way back—cautiously but enthusiastically.

ROCKY KABIR

Rocky Kabir was 31 years old in the spring of 2016 when he met 65-year-old J. David Cox, the then-president of the American Federation of Government Employees (AFGE), the largest federal employee union in the United States with roughly 750,000 members.[4] Rocky worked in an exclusive New York City department store, where he oversaw an account for luxury fragrances. Cox, a fan of such fragrances, would regularly visit the store when he was in New York City. The two formed a friendship and socialized outside of work. Cox even brought Rocky to the Democratic National Convention in Philadelphia, along with AFGE staff.[5]

Initially, Rocky found Cox to be affable, jolly, and friendly. The relationship with Cox—which Rocky saw as a connection to the labor movement—had meaning to Rocky: his father, an immigrant from Bangladesh, left his career as a lawyer and judge behind and began his work life in the United States as a janitor. He had the good fortune of being a member of the local 32BJ of the Service Employees International Union, reportedly the most progressive union in New York. Rocky remembers his father always reminding the family that "32BJ is our insurance, not Blue-Cross Blue-Shield."

Within a few months of meeting Rocky, Cox offered him a job at AFGE headquarters in the President's office in Washington, DC. Rocky was honored and happily accepted the job.

As Cox's "Confidential Secretary," Rocky's primary duties were to assist with scheduling, logistics, and travel with Cox to work meetings and events across the country.

Cox's treatment of Rocky changed when Rocky moved to DC to work for Cox.[6] Rocky, for a time, was living at Cox's apartment at Cox's invitation—a situation that an investigator would later describe as "an arrangement that created vulnerability for [Rocky] Kabir."[7] Cox soon began to subject Rocky to "acts of inappropriate sexual conduct" and to "leverage ... his position of power to make unreasonable and unprofessional demands of [Rocky]."[8]

Cox demanded that Rocky shower with him and often sought physical contact with him, "making repeated attempts to touch his face, private parts, and buttocks."[9] Cox also had

Rocky "accompany him to adult entertainment venues and asked [him] to procure sex workers for him."[10]

Cox was also verbally abusive to Rocky. Witnesses later told investigators that "Cox frequently disparaged Islam, and . . . referred to [Rocky] and others as 'goddamned Muslims.'"[11] Cox was angry and jealous when he found out that Rocky had begun dating someone. When Rocky made clear that he was planning to get married, "Cox began making allegations of poor job performance, and questioning the legitimacy of [Rocky's] timecards, overtime and expense reports."[12]

Rocky left AFGE in 2018. A year later, Rocky told his story to *Bloomberg Businessweek*, which published a wide-ranging exposé of Cox's conduct.[13] Rocky was not the only person who suffered Cox's abuse. The article begins with an anecdote shared by Brett Copeland, a former AFGE staffer: weeks into his dream job, Cox "repeatedly told him he loved him. Then he stuck his tongue in Copeland's ear."[14]

The day the article was published, Cox sent a letter to the union's governing board denying all allegations; the next day, he authorized an investigation, recused himself from it, and took a leave of absence. Four months later, he resigned.[15]

When I asked Rocky what he learned from this experience, he quipped, "With great power comes no responsibility," a playful twist on Spiderman's renowned proverb.[16] "That's why we have to check the people in power," he added. He noted that the systems at play within the union were based on a hierarchy that valued titles and "being part of the circle." As the investigation report summarized, those systems, together with "intimidation and fear by staff of filing complaints against the President, elected officials or other senior leadership," kept victims of harassment and abuse silent for a long time.[17]

Union culture also played a big role in the systemic abuse and the lack of accountability.[18] That culture tolerated heavy drinking by some, including the president and senior leaders, especially at union events or conferences at remote locations or outside typical work hours. Cox made no secret of drinking heavily when he traveled for work.[19] AFGE staff "would warn each other to be wary of Cox late at night or when alcohol or hotel rooms were involved," a former AFGE senior staff person told *Bloomberg News*.[20]

The union hired Jenny R. Yang, a former U.S. Equal Employment Opportunity Commission Chair, to conduct an independent investigation. Yang's scathing report found the following to be credible accounts of Cox's conduct:[21]

- Witnesses reported multiple incidents of Cox talking about soliciting sex workers and/or being asked to procure a sex worker for him.
- Witnesses reported multiple incidents involving Cox staying at a hotel and inviting AFGE staff to his room late at night, sometimes to drink alcohol, watch pornography with him, and/or masturbate with him; Cox was typically intoxicated during these incidents.
- Witnesses reported multiple incidents of Cox becoming angry and screaming at service staff at hotels and airports. In one instance, the behavior was so severe that witnesses reported that it severed the relationship between AFGE and the establishment for a time. One incident involved Cox arriving at an airport intoxicated after a flight, and upon arriving at the hotel, he stood outside and yelled, demanding that a local official come out to greet him.

- Multiple sources described an incident in which Cox allegedly propositioned a member of hotel staff, and hotel management expressed concern to their contacts at AFGE.
- A witness described an incident in which Cox was at a bar with AFGE staff, and Cox asked the group invasive questions about pubic hair grooming.
- A witness described an incident in which Cox made physical contact and a sexual comment while next to an AFGE colleague using a urinal.
- Jane Nygaard [a former AFGE vice president] described an incident that occurred while she was a District National Vice President, in which Cox made a comment about her breast size in front of a group of other members of the [national executive council].

The culture that permitted Cox to continue to act in these shocking ways tolerated the use of racial and religious slurs and inappropriate jokes and comments.[22] The investigation found that Cox and other senior leaders "would joke about sex workers, adult entertainment, sex, physical appearance, and other unprofessional topics."[23]

In addition to the toxic culture, the investigation revealed significant institutional failures: no accountability structures to address misconduct by the president or other elected leadership; senior staff—including lawyers—who were all too happy to look the other way; lack of policies on harassment and discrimination; a void of reporting mechanisms; and organizational structures that discouraged reporting harassment and kept victims silent.

The report included ten detailed recommended actions for the union to address the problems exposed in the report and for the union "to promote a safe, respectful workplace that does not tolerate harassment or other forms of discrimination." Notably, the report recommended that the union work with an outside entity to conduct a culture and climate assessment study and reminded the union that such assessments help prevent harassment and abuse and act as a catalyst for organizational change. In May 2024, this author contacted the union to see what recommendations they had implemented but did not hear back.

Rocky is now working at a different large International Union in Washington, DC, where he is very happy. It was important to Rocky that readers know that his strength to speak up came from his wife and family—and from the #MeToo movement, which taught him that "truth is the only currency that anyone ever needs."

ROXANNE RIFE

Roxanne began her life in the labor movement recording and managing affiliate dues at the Pennsylvania AFL-CIO in November 2019. Roughly a year later, she was promoted to Executive Assistant to the President. She left two years later after suffering humiliating and intolerable treatment from her bosses, the elected leaders.[24] Roxanne saw one of them, Frank Snyder, make every female coworker cry at some point; he also made her and other women feel small regularly. "Frank was always mad—he was always on somebody about something, constantly harassing somebody," Roxanne told *Bloomberg Business News*, "It was terrifying to watch."[25]

Roxanne was forced to endure this dehumanizing treatment while she was being paid $18,000/year less than two male coworkers who reported to her. That is not surprising, given that Rick Bloomingdale, Snyder's co-leader, told Roxanne, "Women belong in clerical roles, not men" and "Women were always supposed to be in clerical roles."[26]

Roxanne had nowhere to turn. She once asked Snyder what room accommodations he preferred during a business trip. A "cheese plate, wine, and twins," he replied. She forwarded the message to Snyder's co-leader, Rick Bloomingdale, expecting him to at least acknowledge the inappropriateness of the message, but Bloomingdale replied with a laughing emoji.[27]

Nor did Roxanne find support from her union. Like many staff jobs in the labor movement, Roxanne's position was covered by a union contract, in her case, Local 1776 of the United Food and Commercial Workers (UFCW). A good union representative will walk new workers through the protections in their contracts and the processes for ensuring that the employer abides by contractual commitments. Roxanne's union representative, Ryan Zarkesh, never did that. She had no idea how to complain against her bosses formally, nor did she understand the imbalance of power that is baked into the relationship between a union and its members.

That's not to say that Zarkesh was absent from her workplace. On the contrary, they became friends—a friendship that she describes as "flirtatious."[28] This writer believes that friendships between union members and their representatives are a natural part of human interaction and are necessary for the union to maintain a strong base of support. However, union representatives must navigate those relationships with caution and transparency because those relationships involve an imbalance of power and can lead to exploitation, which happened here.

One sign that Roxanne's friendship with her union rep was problematic was that Zarkesh asked her to download Signal, a third-party encrypted application on her phone, which she did.[29] Another sign of trouble was that Zarkesh understood Roxanne was working in a toxic environment and took no steps to help her.[30] In one text, he told her, "You work at literally the worst possible employer."[31]

The relationship took a dark turn when Zarkesh drove two hours to Roxanne's home and engaged in inappropriate behavior. After this encounter, Zarkesh sent Roxanne what he called a "Love Contract," a consensual agreement between employees engaged in a sexual relationship, and asked her to sign it quickly, implying his job might be on the line.[32] She did not.

Roxanne also reached out to the national AFL-CIO, hoping Liz Shuler, the federation's first female president, would take her complaints seriously. But instead of hearing from Shuler, she got a response from a lawyer saying the AFL-CIO wasn't responsible for what happened. Then, to top it off, Shuler praised Snyder's "incredible leadership" in a speech just 4 months later. The next day, Snyder was elected president of the Pennsylvania chapter. Shuler's behavior left Rife feeling betrayed, seeing no accountability for those higher up in the organization.

Five months after Roxanne sought Shuler's assistance in dealing with the toxic environment that Snyder created, and one week after Shuler praised his "incredible leadership," Shuler informed the governing body of the Pennsylvania AFL-CIO that the national AFL-CIO would be launching an independent investigation to probe "recent allegations of misconduct."[33] Within a few weeks, Shuler announced that "before the investigation findings were finalized, in order to move the state forward, Snyder decided to retire," which stopped the investigation.[34] No findings or recommendations were ever issued. "It was understood at the AFL-CIO, loyalty matters over issues that we profess to care about, such as racism, sexism, and all of the -isms," Tefere Gebre, the former AFL-CIO executive vice president told *Bloomberg*.[35] "It was known in the building that we're going to look the other way. Pennsylvania is the number one example of that," he continued.

Snyder's bullying behavior was no secret. In 2016, national AFL-CIO staff who were assigned to work in Pennsylvania in relation to the national presidential election filed a grievance against the AFL-CIO under their collective bargaining agreement that included harassment allegations against Snyder. An AFL-CIO supervisor told a reporter that he "witnessed Snyder refer to a woman as a 'fucking bitch,' make another cry, called a man a 'fucking loser,' and described a gay staffer as more interested in performing fellatio than his job duties."[36] That grievance was settled in 2017 when the national AFL-CIO agreed to a complaint procedure for grievances involving harassment and discrimination.

Roxanne filed a complaint against her UFCW union with the local human rights agency.[37] In its response, the union admits that Zarkesh was Roxanne's union representative but maintains that what Zarkesh did to Roxanne was "consensual sex,"[38] which Roxanne staunchly denies.[39] As to the "Love Contract," the UFCW maintains that it is merely its "policy governing consensual intimate relationships in the workplace"[40]—an odd allegation given that the UFCW did not employ Roxanne and thus she would not be bound by the union's HR policies.

In one laughable paragraph of the UFCW's response to Roxanne's legal filing, it refused to admit or deny that Zarkesh had sent Roxanne a text saying that she works for the worst possible employer. According to the union, "Even if he had [sent that text] … the Complainant worked at an employer that allowed her to work half a day on Fridays during the summer, provided a Platinum healthcare plan, and a pension."[41]

Roxanne now lives in South America, where she has found peace. She told me that she stood up to Snyder because she knew the other women in her office could not risk being fired. "I didn't have children, and I could leave. I wanted to make sure that other women don't go through what I and the women I worked with went through."[42]

VALENTINA[43]

Valentina is an experienced union organizer, educator, and negotiator who embodies strength and resilience. As a survivor of sexual violence, her antennae are synchronized to those who need help. Empathy is in her DNA.

In 2018, she was hired into a senior position dealing with collective bargaining in a union that represents professionals in the media industry. The union was under the #MeToo spotlight at the time and received praise for the way it spoke about sexual harassment. Valentina was surprised when she learned that the union had no language on sexual harassment or racial equity in its contracts, and she set out to bargain such language, which she did.

Members at one of the bargaining units she oversaw, along with a colleague, Nick, reported rampant sexual harassment and asked what the union was going to do about it. At that time, the contract provided nothing more than a process for a group of union members and management representatives to meet and talk about it (a so-called Labor-Management Committee). She attended one of those meetings and learned that the meeting had been called because Nick was being investigated for sexual harassment. A week earlier, after a meeting on a separate topic, Nick, along with some union members, went to a bar where Nick bought rounds of drinks (with the union credit card). A young female member, who Valentina describes as 25 years old and weighing no more than 95 pounds, had three large old fashioneds (a cocktail), and Nick put his hand on her leg and propositioned her. The woman left.

Valentina later talked to the shop steward about Nick. As is often the case, the woman was worried that Nick would lose his job or be reassigned; she felt guilty about that. But, when she learned that he would remain overseeing her unit, she started to have panic attacks. The union removed Nick from those contract negotiations.

When Valentina heard about what Nick had done, she went to the general counsel, asking what she was going to do about Nick. The lawyer replied that she had known Nick for seven years, and he'd never do something like that. No accountability.

Valentina then went to the executive director of the union, an older white man. He told her that what Nick did was not a fireable offense. Valentina reminded the executive director that Nick was hitting on members after buying drinks with the union's credit card, and she wondered, how is that not a fireable offense? He told her that Nick had been there for eleven years, he's a dad, he's divorced—and sexual harassment was not just cause to fire someone. No accountability.

Valentina also turned to the organizing director, who didn't want to get involved. Again, no accountability.

Valentina had sympathy for Nick. She had been sober for nearly two decades at the time, and she told the general counsel that it would help Nick to hold him accountable. That's what had helped her: she had been called out for drinking and knew that she couldn't bullshit people. Boundaries helped her. She also offered to find some restorative justice approach to hold Nick accountable, but there was no interest in that either.

Valentina had to explain that she didn't have a vendetta against Nick; she was concerned about the members' safety. She and a woman colleague had heard about Nick's behavior, and they knew that their members were young and easily influenced, especially by alcohol. Nick had recently been in Chicago bargaining a contract with a unit composed of twenty-somethings. They went to a happy hour where the same pattern occurred. All her concerns and ideas fell on deaf ears.

Nick left the union within months. The staff received an email saying he no longer worked there, period. No explanation. No systems change.

The fallout was a nightmare for Valentina. She was labeled a troublemaker. The staff union (which was under the control of the head of the union) filed a grievance against her for bullying. She felt tension in the office, which seriously impacted her mental health. While she had no institutional support, she had something stronger: the members loved her. She was able to negotiate an exit package and now works for another union headed by a strong, powerful, down-to-earth woman, and she is very happy.

Her experience reinforced her belief that unions need to put members first—not a banal truism. Valentina's time at this union showed that members wanted and needed change. They wanted the union to live up to its public statements about sexual harassment. Instead, in her view, union staff prioritized their personal interests. When I asked her what this experience taught her, she replied, "There are too many careerists in the labor movement." "The status quo favors white people who lack creativity and imagination. They're trying to keep what they have and not lose what they want."[44]

These stories bring to life the theory of *institutional betrayal*—a term in psychology that refers to the trauma that institutions cause when they fail to uphold their duty of care, protection, or trust towards their members.[45] Each of these brave souls believed that their unions would come to their aid, and each was betrayed in different ways. These stories should serve as a catalyst for unions to critically change their course on how they handle sexual harassment and ensure that these experiences remain relics of the past, not the lived experiences of others.

4

The Enablers: Law and Culture

> You cannot solve a problem from the same consciousness that created it.
>
> —Albert Einstein

For decades, society did not consider sexual harassment a systemic issue. At best, it was seen as the actions of a few bad actors; at worst, it was treated as a joke and often blamed on the poor sense of humor or the actions of the survivor.[1] That belief is changing: today, 66 percent of Americans believe that sexual harassment represents a widespread problem in society, while only 28 percent attribute individual conduct as the problem.[2] The journalist Christiane Amanpour summarized it well to the Committee to Protect Journalists in 2017:

> It is important that powerful serial harassers are taken down. But these were not the only men responsible: There were executives who made calculations of money or convenience, HR departments that were unresponsive or untrusting, and lawyers who drafted non-disclosure agreements to keep women silent. We need to widen the lens and recognize that this is not a problem of a few bad apples.[3]

What is enabling this collective harm that denigrates and harms women and other marginalized workers? Or, as the U.S. Equal Opportunity Commission asked in 2016, "With legal liability long ago established, reputational harm from harassment well known, and an entire industry of workplace compliance and training in place for 30 years, why does so much harassment persist in so many of our workplaces?"[4]

There is no easy answer. The investigation into misconduct by AFGE's former president, J. David Cox, revealed multiple interlocking forces that fostered an environment where Cox's conduct went unchecked.[5] One of the most prominent was the union's culture.[6] Indeed, research shows that organizational culture plays a major role in facilitating or enabling harassment.[7] Cultures that are inclusive, diverse, and communitarian and do not tolerate bullying and harassment offer the most protection against sexual harassment.[8]

LABOR CULTURE

It is no secret that unions operate in a hyper-masculinist culture historically rooted in struggle and conflict, primarily shaped by white men.[9] In the words of Marion Crain and Ken Matheny, "Incubated in bars and taverns and permeated with language such as 'brothers' and 'brotherhood,' male labor did not construct unionism as either accessible or comfortable for women."[10] And as Lin Farley, one of the pioneers in the fight against sexual harassment and the person who coined the term "sexual harassment," put it,

> The mainstream of the American labor movement was fueled at birth by a desire to maintain the male domination of female labor; the very heartbeat of this movement's unions is male rights.[11]

Traditions, customs, iconography, and physical spaces of many unions continue to reflect periods when unions openly practiced sexism and racism. "Buildings, scholarships, and awards are named after the male heroes. It is the faces of male unionists which line the walls."[12] The most beautiful room at the AFL-CIO, with its 20-foot ceilings and framed by Lumen Winter's beautiful mosaic mural of glass, marble, and gold, is named after Samuel Gompers who believed that "a woman's place is in the home" and who, in his memoir, expressed his belief in "the principle that maintenance of the nation depended upon maintenance of racial purity."[13]

Unions have staunchly defended this culture, especially in male-dominated industries like mining, construction, and manufacturing.[14] For example, in defending the discharge of a miner who over the course of two and a half years, called his female coworker "a lazy bitch," "*vieja pinche puta*," swung his clenched fists at her as if to strike her, repeatedly made obscene gestures towards her, and stalked her, the union "emphasized that a workplace such as a mine/mill is not a parlor room," and that "it is commonplace for the rougher edges of humanity to be revealed in such a site."[15]

This attitude is not a relic of history. A 2022 arbitration decision that reads like a script from *The Office* describes what a rookie firefighter experienced on his first day on the job in a Florida fire station. When the rookie, Rob, returned from a dispatched call, a fellow firefighter, Greg, told Rob that he had placed his genitalia on food Rob had brought for lunch.[16] Rob thought this was a joke, and continued eating his lunch. Greg told Rob that it was not a joke, and Rob threw his lunch away.[17]

The crew later sat down for dinner and began discussing what Greg had done with his genitalia at lunch. Greg told the table, "To be correct, it was 'one ball' and not balls as he only has one." The discussion then focused on Greg's one testicle and "the circumstances and procedures that led to [Greg] having one testicle." After "being egged on to show his one testicle," Greg stood up, turned towards Rob, unzipped his pants, and exposed himself.[18] Greg was fired for "exposure of his scrotum."[19] The union grieved.

In defense of Greg's conduct, the union argued that "conduct in firehouses has been recognized … as generally rife with teasing, horseplay, sexual organ display, and similar antics."[20] Yes, the union wants us to believe that it is totally normal for men who put out fires for a living to display their sexual organs at work. In support of that notion, the union submitted a photograph of a firefighter in uniform, standing slightly behind a fire lieutenant, "exposing his testicles and scrotum."[21]

The rookie testified that he was offended by Greg's actions. The union, following the patriarchal playbook, tried to minimize the victim's experience and make much of the fact that the rookie played ping pong with Greg and others after dinner. Fortunately, the arbitrator rejected that argument and recognized that the rookie was just trying to fit in at a new station where his future was in the hands of others in the room.[22]

LABOR LAW

Hyper-masculine culture is also embedded in labor law. For example, the National Labor Relations Board (NLRB or Board), the entity that enforces the U.S. federal labor code, maintains a doctrine known as the "realities of industrial life." That doctrine is based on a 1950s version of the workplace where vulgarity, profanity, and sexist and racist language are normal, accepted, everyday occurrences otherwise known as "shop talk."

The Board has explained that "tempers may run high in this emotional field, that the language of the shop is not the language of 'polite society,' and that tolerance of some deviation from that which might be the most desirable behavior is required."[23] Thus, only activities that are "so flagrant, violent, or extreme as to render the individual unfit for further service" will be deemed unprotected.[24]

Under this reasoning, a union defended a man discharged after he constantly referred to a female coworker as "bitch" or "fat ass"; frequently grabbed at her breasts; often greeted her with "Do you want to fuck?"; often asked her "Who'd you fuck last night?"; made remarks on sex positions; sometimes grabbed his crotch, shook it at her, and asked, "Hungry?"; and pulled off her shirt to look at her breasts. The union's position was that this conduct was "nothing more than shop talk," and that "the grievant's use of the word 'bitch' [was] his ordinary means of addressing females, including his wife."[25] While disputes between labor and capital might (and do) provoke "high tempers," the law has developed such as to provide an excuse for expressions of misogyny.

Unions also rely on the doctrine of "horseplay" as a means to avoid accountability for the harm caused by hyper-masculine (and racist) behavior on the job. Professor Marion Crain has cataloged cases where unions—sometimes with the approval of an arbitrator—defend misogynistic behavior as horseplay.[26] Unions' versions of horseplay include locking a woman in a supply closet, wrestling her down to a couch, and trying to remove her clothes—a near rape, as well as an incident where three male employees grabbed a female employee from behind, held her off the floor, and pulled at her clothing while one grievant said to the other two, "Let's get her, guys."[27] Unions have not abandoned this doctrine: in a fairly recent case involving a white union member who tied a noose and dropped it in the toolbox of the only Black worker at the facility, the union defended the behavior as nothing more than "horseplay."[28]

Relatedly, labor law treats strikes as manifestations of masculinity. The NLRB analyzes conduct on the picket line through an overly masculine lens, which draws a line between "animal exuberance" (permissible conduct) and conduct that "is so violent or of such serious character as to render the employee unfit for further service."[29] Thus, the Board has held that a striker calling a non-striker a "whore" and a "prostitute" and adding that she was "having sex with [the employer's] president" was not "serious misconduct" and thus was not sanctionable.[30] That same striker repeatedly called a second female employee "a 'whore' and told [her] she could earn more money by selling her daughter, another nonstriker, at the flea market," which the Board also deemed within the bounds of the law.[31] The Board has further deemed it acceptable for a striker to yell at female non-strikers to "come see a real man" and then to "pull ... down his pants and expose ... himself"; it also ordered the reinstatement of a striker who "made crude and obscene remarks and suggestions regarding sex, including an invitation to 'make some extra money at his apartment that night'" to a female employee.[32] Unions continue to advance this doctrine today. For example, a union recently argued that a member who shouted "Fucking dyke!" at two female non-striking employees while holding his fingers in a "V" shape and sticking his tongue between his fingers was engaged in protected conduct, not subject to discipline.[33]

Implicit in the "realities of industrial life," "shop talk," "horseplay," and "animal exuberance" doctrines is the notion that "boys will be boys." Importantly, these hyper-masculine doctrines and the practices that flow from them put women workers at risk, which is the opposite of what labor law is meant to do.[34]

THE DUTY OF FAIR REPRESENTATION: UNIONS' SHIELD TO ACCOUNTABILITY

Hyper-masculinist cultures have shaped the way unions respond to claims of coworker sexual harassment, which is the most common type of sexual harassment.[35] Typically, when one union member accuses another of sexual harassment, the following scenario unfolds: a woman reports sexual harassment by a coworker to the union representative. Instead of filing a formal grievance on the victim's behalf, the representative refers her to HR—an unnecessary and often further traumatizing step for the survivor, essentially washing his hands of the complaint.[36] The employer conducts the investigation and disciplines the accused when finding actionable harassment. The union then defends the harasser by filing a grievance and invoking the protections in the collective bargaining agreement, effectively making the victim a witness for the employer and pitting her against the union.

In some cases, the union actively discourages the victim from filing a grievance.[37] A recent academic review of labor arbitration awards involving sexual harassment found no grievances filed by victims of sexual harassment; in other words, all the grievances challenged the punishment inflicted on union members accused of harassment.[38]

Unions justify this dynamic by citing an exaggerated interpretation of their duty to represent all members fairly.[39] "The law requires that I fight the harasser's discipline" is a common—but incorrect—explanation. The law grants unions significant leeway in deciding whether to process a grievance;

a study found that members who sue their unions are successful in only 5 percent of cases.[40] To successfully sue a union for breaching its duty of fair representation, an employee must prove arbitrary or bad-faith conduct by the union in processing their grievance. The standard "gives the union room to make discretionary decisions and choices even if those judgments are ultimately wrong."[41] Assuming the union conducts a good-faith investigation and notifies members, it can decide what to do next, including not processing a grievance.

Unions often face competing claims from members; for example, disputes over promotions are not uncommon, with senior and junior bidders claiming superior skill or ability. Courts have consistently held that a union "may take a position in favor of one ... employee only on the basis of an informed, reasoned judgment regarding the merits of the claim."[42] Therefore, a union that conducts a fair investigation and concludes harassment occurred "has no duty to represent members for discipline they incurred for engaging in sexually or racially harassing conduct."[43] Yet citing their fair representation duty is often how unions justify defending harassers.

Defending harassers while sending the survivor to HR harms both the victim and the union, as it marginalizes a member when they are most vulnerable and negatively impacts morale and solidarity. Importantly, it creates a disincentive for reporting: union women who observe the consequences of reporting harassment understandably choose not to undergo the same process. This is particularly concerning given that over 75 percent of sexual harassment victims do not report the harassment.[44]

In the wake of #MeToo, labor lawyers offered a slew of ideas for legal reform intended to prevent sexual harassment. They included banning non-disclosure agreements (which silence survivors), modifying anti-discrimination laws, strengthening whistle-blower and anti-retaliation protections, and criminally prosecuting workplace violations when appropriate.[45] None of the commentaries included changes to labor law or union practices.

In 2019, unions had an opportunity to influence how labor law could help shift workplace culture away from the "rough-and-tumble" masculinist dynamics that current law and practice encourage towards a more feminist approach. That year, the NLRB invited answers to the question, "Under what circumstances should sexually or racially offensive speech lose the protection of the Act?"[46] Unions universally defended such speech by promoting the same masculinist norms where tempers flaring, profanity, and racist language are considered acceptable at all costs. The AFL-CIO's brief argued that unions "need license to use intemperate, abusive, or insulting language without fear of restraint or penalty if it believes such rhetoric to be an effective means to make its point … Unfortunately, this sometimes includes the use of racially and sexually derogatory and charged language."[47]

While positive developments in the law in this area have been slow, there is some good news. Individual complaints of sexual harassment weren't recognized as a collective harm protected by the labor law until 2014.[48] Until then, the Board held that, where one employee is the alleged victim, that lone employee's protest is not protected by the labor law, even if the victim seeks support from other employees. According to the Board, "The bare possibility that the second employee may one day suffer similar treatment, and may herself seek help, is far too speculative a basis on which to rest a finding of mutual aid or protection."[49] More than 80 percent of working women experience sexual harassment; there is clearly more than a speculative likelihood that another employee will suffer harassment.

Neither law nor culture is static. Unions don't have to wait for legal reform to change their practices. Tools are available to help change cultures. Climate assessments are critical, and some unions are starting to explore them. As you will see in the next chapter, the California janitor's local, United Service Workers West (USWW), is using state laws to facilitate culture change through member education, and changing internal practices on how they handle allegations of harassment by one member against another to ensure that all members work in an environment free of harassment. Nothing is stopping other unions from following suit.

An easy way for unions to begin the process of change is to stop feeding into sexist paradigms like horseplay and "animal exuberance." Those are not only juvenile. They cause real harm.

UNION STRUCTURES

Masculinist cultures of sexism do not exist in a vacuum. Despite substantial efforts by women around the world towards gender equality, men continue to control union leadership positions and structures, a phenomenon that Geraldine Healy and Gill Kirton call "gendered oligarchies."[50] According to the International Labour Organization (ILO), women currently account for only 28 percent of the membership of the highest decision-making bodies of trade unions globally.[51] In the United States, women make up approximately half the workforce, yet remain substantially underrepresented in union leadership in most unions.[52] Women make up 19.1 percent of the AFL-CIO's executive council, which is notably lower than women's overall representation in union membership, which stands at 46.8 percent of the unionized workforce in the United States.[53] To put it simply, when women don't have a voice in leadership, patriarchal practices persist.

There has been progress in the last decade. For example, the International Trade Union Confederation (ITUC) Constitution, adopted in 2006 and most recently revised in 2018, mandates women's rights, gender equality, gender parity in all leadership bodies and the full participation of women trade unionists at all levels. At the 2018 ITUC Congress, the global trade union movement set a target of a minimum 40 percent representation of women in leadership positions.[54]

While I do not pretend to cover the depth and scope that gender equality in unions deserves, I raise the issue because the common wisdom has been that if more women were in leadership positions, trade unions would advance gender equality with more vigor. Researchers continue to debate that question. There is no simple answer. As the historian Dorothy Sue Cobble reminds us in her critical review of the English-language research on gender equality and labor movements, "of course, as with union feminization, the addition of more women to the union executive suite by itself is no guarantee the union will increase its commitment to a program of gender equality, particularly if women remain tokens."[55]

There is a consensus, however, that gender parity alone is not enough to address culture problems within unions. While achieving equal representation is important, it must be part of a comprehensive approach that addresses deeply rooted cultural issues, power dynamics, and structural inequalities within unions.

5

Rays of Hope

My mission from day one was to get rid of the fucking word "can't."

—United Auto Workers (UAW)
president Shawn Fain, 2024

Labor unions, like most institutions, are slow to adapt to change. It took time for unions to recognize women, Black workers, and immigrants as part of the labor movement. For decades, the AFL-CIO refused to take a position on abortion, yielding "to the good and sound judgment of union members … that they choose to pursue their goals on reproductive issues within political, legislative and legal arenas as their individual consciences dictate."[1] Although the word abortion appears nowhere in any current AFL-CIO policy statements, the federation passed a resolution at its 25th Biennial Convention in 2012 that promotes "contraceptive equity in national health plans and collective bargaining agreements."[2] And at least one union, the News Guild/Communication Workers of America, has developed model contract language that deals directly with abortion as well as other reproductive health issues.[3] Unions have also made progress in recognizing that workers organize in various ways, some of which don't lead to collective bargaining. Not long ago, many unions saw "alt-labor"—also known as workers centers—as a threat, and now some are working closely with this emerging labor movement of immigrants and marginalized workers.[4]

When it comes to addressing sexual harassment, we are seeing the beginning stages of progress and promising practices.

The shining star is the United Service Workers West (USWW) chapter of the Service Employees International Union (SEIU), representing California janitors. The union's janitorial membership includes a large number of immigrant women working in isolation in high-rise buildings at night. The bosses—foremen, leads, supervisors, and contractors—are all men.[5] This combination creates a significant risk that the janitors will face assault or harassment.[6]

The public narrative of how USWW made confronting sexual harassment a union priority begins with the documentary *Rape on the Nightshift*, a shocking exposé of what immigrant women janitors routinely faced on the job.[7] The documentary features first-hand accounts from the janitors who recount being sexually assaulted, groped, or raped by male coworkers and supervisors.[8] At internal union screenings of the documentary, members shared their own stories of sexual harassment and violence.[9]

Women in leadership knew that members were deeply affected by the issue. Alejandra Valles, the Secretary-Treasurer of USWW, shared the heartbreaking story of a woman that she worked with who "was forcefully assaulted with her own broomstick and didn't realize that a crime had been committed against her because, as she put it, 'in my upbringing that is not considered intercourse, you can't get pregnant so it's treated as if nothing happened.'"[10]

While the documentary was important in shedding light on the problem, the union's effort to confront sexual harassment started much earlier. The story is an essential reminder that institutional change requires multiple levels of intervention. The janitors' story is actually a story of culture change, collective action, legislative change, and, most importantly, worker leadership and self-empowerment.

Key to this effort were two high-ranking Latina staff members, Alejandra Valles and Sandra Diaz, both of whom are now in elected leadership positions. Alejandra is a survivor of rape; when she and Sandra came to work at the local in the late 1990s, they were met with a culture of machismo–not uncommon in the southern California labor movement.[11]

Bonds among staff and leaders were often forged in one local bar where everything was "two for one," which led to much drinking. Potential leaders and senior staff were tested there to see if they were "*firme*," a Spanish word with multiple meanings. In Mexican-American slang, it denotes qualities like strength and toughness, reinforcing societal expectations of being a man. It also has sexual connotations; to be "*firme*" is to have an erection. At the bar—and in the union—"*firme*" defined a culture where men could make sexual jokes around women, "where boys could be boys."[12]

"There was also male camaraderie in that space, and lots of talk about campaigns and work—strategizing on paper napkins." The test of those aspiring to rise to leadership "wasn't whether you went against it; it was whether you could roll with it."[13] Once, an aspiring director took off her bra and started waving it around to show that she was "*firme*."

Alejandra and Sandra initially worked under the leadership of Mike Garcia, the iconic president of SEIU Local 1877 and USWW, and one of the prominent leaders of the Justice for Janitors Campaign. "Mike was a good guy, but the culture of the local had been built around older men—lots of sexism," Sandra told me.[14]

Garcia was a strong supporter of immigration reform and pushed the International Union to become more involved in efforts to achieve legislative change at the national level. The failing U.S. immigration system had left 11 million undocumented workers and their families toiling in the shadows of oppression; the workers were of great concern to Garcia. For the local to engage on the issue of immigration effectively, the membership needed to be fully supportive. To get there, Garcia began an organizational drive centered on racial equity, which focused on "building across differences rather than finding common ground."[15] The project's goal became to "identify the values we want to keep, the values we want to grow, and the ones we want to kick to the curb." That process required hard and painful conversations.

Gender bubbled up as an issue during those conversations. It took center stage at an executive board meeting that included members, elected leaders, and staff, where a facilitator led an exercise commonly known as "Stand Up If." The facilitator instructs everyone to sit and then reads a series of statements about different identities or experiences. For example, "Stand up if you were born outside of this country," or "Stand up if you've been stopped by the police while driving." The exercise aims to identify shared experiences and highlight unique experiences within the group.

When the facilitator said, "Stand up if you are a survivor of sexual violence, almost every woman in the room stood up, as well as a man," Alejandra told me. "It was a huge moment; it shook everyone." That moment created the space for the union to combat sexual violence and harassment comprehensively. It also provided the opportunity for the members, staff, and leadership to take on the culture of "*firme.*" It was on the "kick to the curb" list.[16]

Following that meeting, in preparation for a new round of contract negotiations, the leadership circulated a survey that would help identify members' priorities. Sexual violence and harassment ranked second in the members' priorities, behind only wages, a result that surprised the elected leaders, putting sexual harassment squarely on the bargaining table.

USWW worked closely with the Maintenance Cooperation Trust Fund (MCTF), a union-adjacent non-profit organization whose aim is to hold accountable "bottom feeders" in the industry—those who profit from flouting wage, labor, safety and health, environmental, and other laws. Together, they began to address harassment as a union issue, using various tools in the union toolbox.

Women janitors were at the forefront of the union's efforts. Storytelling was crucial to their effort. One particularly impactful example consists of letters that the women wrote to their rapists and abusers. According to Alejandra, the letters were cathartic for the women. Many reported realizing that the person responsible for their trauma was the abuser, not themselves, which was liberating.

One of the first steps the union and MCTF took was to craft a campaign to pass legislation that would protect all workers in the janitorial industry. The union advocated for a bill called the Property Service Workers Protection Act (AB 1978), which required that employers provide preventative sexual harassment training to their employees and contractors.[17] The janitors and their allies won the legislation when the women engaged in a hunger strike in the summer of 2016. Four days into the strike, the Governor of California signed the bill.[18]

Around this same time, the union created the *Ya Basta!* (Spanish for "enough is enough!") coalition, which includes local anti-rape organizations, the Occupational Safety and Health Project at the University of California, Los Angeles, Cornell University's School of Industrial Labor Relations,

Equal Rights Advocates, and MCTF. Alejandra recalls that Sandra's and her top priority at the time was "to make sure that the work is here to stay," in other words, that it would be institutionalized.[19]

From the very beginning, they made sure that the effort was worker-led and trauma-informed: "Everything had to come from the members."[20] "Without doing the work internally with the members, members would have known that it wasn't authentic."[21] This is why the internal organizational equity work was so important to the effort. Alejandra recalls that staff recognized that they needed to "lead from the back, and men stepped aside." The process included difficult, inward-looking reflections with the members. Together, they kicked "*firme*" to the curb.

The union developed a worker-centered peer-to-peer leadership and education approach based on the popular education philosophy of the Brazilian educator Paulo Freire: the workers designed the curriculum and became certified under Cornell University's Institutional Review Board (IRB) to conduct research involving human subjects.[22] The campaign developed a trauma-informed methodology that relies on community peer ed—*promotoras*—who go into workplaces to share knowledge and resources with fellow workers to continue the work on the ground. The approach was modeled on efforts crafted by social justice medical doctors and public health experts in southern California who trained community members to advance healthy practices within the community. To date, over a hundred *promotoras* have been certified as trainers.[23]

The effort started with 13 *promotoras*. The curriculum begins with the women understanding their own experience through the lens of patriarchy. A *promotora* told me that she experienced a fundamental change in her life: she was able to confront her husband regarding his notion that women are responsible for their assault, that they "ask for it." To her surprise, her husband did not leave. She felt the shame that she had been carrying for years "fly away."[24]

The peer-to-peer education model is one of the most significant innovations in combating sexual harassment at a workplace that includes vulnerable women. That model was sealed into law in 2019 with the passage of the California Janitor Survivor Empowerment Act, which built on the janitors' earlier legislative victory.[25] Under the new law, janitors themselves must conduct the training, and the employer must compensate them for doing so. "The hardest part of getting this law passed was to convince the world that janitors are the experts," Alejandra said. "People would not believe that janitors who can't read or write can teach," she continued.[26] Not only can they teach, but janitors have become agents of change.

The brilliance of this model lies in the fact that it uses legislation as a catalyst for cultural change. "Janitors walk in the front door and they get paid for educating each other."[27] This is not about tweaking the law so that more victims can bring lawsuits; it's about changing the whole system.

In 2016, after the janitors' first legislative victory, the union opened the *Ya Basta!* Center, which provides *promotoras* a space to engage with fellow workers, educate them on their legal rights and self-empowerment, and continue training the janitorial community to confront and eradicate sexual harassment on the job.[28] It is a serene space, with lavender walls, comfortable chairs, and artwork that depicts the janitors' struggles and victories.

The Center also operates as a way to engage janitors as unionists across borders. Veronica, a janitor and mother of two who left El Salvador after an earthquake hit her country, said it beautifully:[29]

> I believe we can start spreading [this program]. We grad-
> uated as trainers to be able to give this type of training in
> workplaces. Honestly, I see myself in the future going to
> other industries and telling them, "This is what we were
> going through, and this is how we overcame it. So now we
> want to give this model to other industries." ... This *pro-
> motora* program can be expanded because it works ...
> Ultimately, I want to have a *Ya Basta!* Center in my home
> country [of El Salvador] because I see the need there. I was
> invited to give a workshop there, and the union leaders were
> all so interested in the work we're doing. They asked, "So is
> this something we can apply here in El Salvador?" and I said
> "Yes!" And they asked who could give them training—well,
> here I am. So, I see a future in which I'm helping the women
> in my country.

As evidence of structural change, the union quietly altered the way it processes grievances regarding sexual harassment. It bargained language that breaks the harmful practice of sending survivors to HR while the union defends the harasser. The new collectively bargained process states that upon receiving notice of sexual harassment, the employer will conduct an investiga-tion, and "[t]he union will support the Employer's decision in this regard consistent with the duty of fair representation."[30] In other words, if the union believes the investigation and the punishment to be fair, it will not take up a harasser's grievance.

The union's continuing success offers a powerful blueprint for the kind of real-world progress that unions can achieve when a union fully commits its resources to campaigns led by sexual assault survivors and immigrant women of color. The union's internal work to address its "*firme*" culture was essential—and rare. As Alejandra recognized, without that work, the members would not have seen the efforts as genuine. After all, unions are democratic institutions and like any democracy, they are only effective with the participation and consent of its citizens.

Sexual harassment has also been one of the driving forces behind the upsurge in graduate student organizing.[31] This is not surprising given the alarming rate of sexual harassment in academia: a prominent study found that 58 percent of female academic faculty and staff have experienced sexual harassment.[32] A climate survey conducted in 2019 by the Association of American Universities (AAU) revealed that nearly a quarter (24 percent) of graduate and professional women who reported being harassed were harassed by a faculty member or instructor.[33]

Dr. Karen Kelsky created an anonymous open-sourced survey of sexual harassment in the academy. Within a month, the survey reached more than 2500 entries. "It makes for sickening reading," her website notes.[34]

Graduate students are especially susceptible to harassment because they occupy a vulnerable position within the entrenched hierarchical structure of academic institutions. As Dr. Kelsky describes, "the male dominance of virtually every field other than women's studies, the culture of collegiality (read, evasiveness and pretense) that predominates, and junior scholar's desperate dependency on good references for career advancement, make for conditions in which sexual abuse (and indeed abuse of all kinds) can flourish with impunity." The risks of abuse are higher for non-cis white female students: a 2021 study of sexual harassment in academia found that "being a female student with an LGBTQIA+ identity was the strongest predictor of harassment and women who identified as a racial minority experienced harassment at the intersection of these inextricably linked identities."[35] International students are also vulnerable to abuse because they cannot walk away from an abusive job because they would jeopardize their visa status. This is not a small problem. Some universities are increasingly recruiting international students because they can charge higher tuition; at least 15 percent of U.S. graduate students in 2023 were foreign born.[36]

An internal 2015 survey found that nearly 70 percent of female graduate students at Harvard believed that they would face retaliation by the offender or his associates if they reported sexual misconduct, and over a quarter believed that retaliation was either "very" or "somewhat" likely. In five out of ten cases, the harassment was by a faculty member.[37]

Universities are also neoliberal institutions, where market logic predominates.[38] In the crass terms of capitalism, tenured faculty are worth more than graduate students: they bring money, publicity, and prestige to the university. Graduate students simply bring their labor.[39]

As Ege Yumusak, one of the leaders of the Harvard University organizing campaign, explained in relation to the union's 2019 strike, "our stipend, which is subject to unexpected changes, barely keeps up with the cost of living in Cambridge; we lack year-round mental health resources, dental coverage, and child support."[40] Yet, she points out, "the most pressing issue for many picketers was not low pay or inadequate healthcare, but the university's handling of sexual harassment cases."[41]

Students at all universities in the United States that receive federal funding—whether public or private—are protected from sex-based discrimination, including sexual harassment by federal law, Title IX of the Education Amendments of 1972 (Title IX)—at least in theory.[42] Universities have adopted a maze of policies and protocols to comply with Title IX, mostly tailored to limit their own liability and protect their reputation—at the expense of students.[43] The processes, which are crafted in secret and fully under the control of the university, start with intake coordinators, who frequently discourage students from speaking up ("maybe you should wait until you get tenure") and sometimes even misinform students about their rights.[44] Students who wish to pursue a formal complaint must deal with multiple layers of bureaucracy and rules that exacerbate the trauma that they've experienced as a result of the harassment. Most universities do not keep the survivor's name confidential; the process has become overly legalistic, reminiscent of the television drama *Law and Order*, where misogynistic attitudes judge and demean women. Harvard's archaic practices fail to credit survivors' complaints unless they are corroborated by independent evidence, a standard that many survivors cannot meet.[45]

The problem is not limited to U.S. universities. In her groundbreaking book, *Complaint!*, Sara Ahmed pinpointed the issue exactly: "Making a complaint can require becoming an institutional mechanic: you have to work out how to get a complaint through the system. It is because of the difficulty of getting complaints through the system that complaints often end up about the system."[46]

In light of these obstacles, graduate students turned to organizing a union with the goal of securing sexual harassment and assault protections and a third-party accountability system for the university. In other words, they want to be able to address sexual harassment through a collectively bargained grievance process instead of the Title IX processes.

At Harvard University, the organizing effort swelled when the organizing campaign took on sexual harassment. A few months before students voted for representation by UAW Local 5118, reports surfaced that Government Professor Jorge Dominguez had sexually harassed as many as 18 undergraduate and graduate students over the course of 30 years. The campaign's messaging shifted from traditional bread-and-butter issues to sexual harassment and assault protections, and the possibility of third-party accountability for the university.[47]

Organizers formed a feminist working group, the Time's Up Committee, which became the center of the campaign.[48] It has continued to play a key role in educating students about their rights, organizing students to urge the university to take concrete, effective action to end harassment across campus, and serving as a space where women can speak out about sexual violence on campus.[49]

The union won the election in 2018, and the campaign shifted to securing anti-harassment protections and a grievance process at the bargaining table. More than 2000 student workers signed a petition demanding a contract with harassment protections, which was delivered at a rally; organizers reported that the rally radicalized many of them, inspiring them to join and take leadership in the campaign.[50]

The union secured a hard-fought contract in 2019, after a year of negotiations. Following the failure of the parties to come to agreements on key provisions, including health care, compensation, and sexual harassment and discrimination grievance procedures, the union was forced to strike. The parties eventually agreed to the economic terms, and some positive provisions on sexual harassment (described below), but the university refused to budge on the third-party reporting mechanism. The union was forced to strike again in 2021 in support of its second contract; while that strike was resolved in three days, the university again refused to budge on third-party reporting.

The contracts secured by the union address some of the flaws in Harvard's system but not all. On the positive side, Harvard is required to provide all complainants a letter from the union that outlines the various avenues of recourse, the right to union representation and contact information for the union. The contract also specifies that "under no circumstances should a [complainant] be pressured by Title IX Resource Coordinators or staff or any other University Officials to accept informal resolution of their complaint or supportive measures, in place of filing a formal complaint," giving examples of pressure like "telling the [complainant] that they will not win a formal resolution, providing misinformation about the formal resolution process, and telling the complainant that the resolution process will harm the academic opportunities of the respondent." The contract also gives complainants and the union a voice as to who sits on appeals panels; an important provision of the contract concerns "supportive measures" for victims, which can be implemented as soon as a complaint (even if informal) is filed. Those measures may include no-contact orders, changing the accused to a different work station, leave time, change of supervisor, and others intended to permit the complainant to continue campus life as normally as possible. Retaliation is also prohibited, as is deliberately providing false or misleading information. The union intends to keep fighting for a third-party reporting system.

Graduate students at other universities are on the same path. In its 2023–26 contract, MIT graduate students won the right for any graduate student to have a union representative at all of the university's formal complaint procedures.[51] At Georgetown University, the graduate student union secured improved anti-harassment measures in their first contract ratified in 2020, which the union president cited as an important achievement of organizing, even though the union was not able to secure a contractually governed harassment system.[52] The union at the University of California system negotiated provisions in their 2022 contract to strengthen protections against bullying and abusive conduct, including sexual harassment and discrimination. This included an agreement to form a joint union-management committee to address these issues.[53] At the University of Massachusetts, the graduate employee union's 2021 contract established clearer procedures for reporting harassment and discrimination, as well as protections against retaliation for those who file complaints.

There is a lot to learn from graduate students as they work to address sexual harassment through unionization. Ege Yumusak shared her analysis at a conference at the National Center for the Study of Collective Bargaining in Higher Education in 2023: "In higher education, harassment and discrimination are rampant and systemic. In this landscape, real recourse achieved through collective bargaining is urgent, but insufficient."[54] Ege and her Local 5118 siblings shared fundamental advice for unions: they must win the trust of survivors before incorporating harassment into a campaign. "Without the trust of survivors, campaigns cannot set a clear narrative and cannot achieve hard wins."[55] In order to win that trust, the union must build a working group, enter into coalition work with existing organizations, and create a community of activists/experts before entering into bargaining.[56] They also concluded that "unions are unprepared to lead" at the moment. Dealing with harassment requires "1) expanding the understanding of grievance to involve community care, 2) protecting sensitive information by trusting a single grievance officer, 3) growing capacity by effective recruitment from vulnerable groups and supporting grievance officers to handle incredibly time-consuming and emotional [harassment] cases without burnout."[57]

This advice is remarkably similar to the janitor's union's approach: do the internal work necessary to prepare the union to fully grasp the workers' experiences with sexual harassment and violence; look outward to build relationships with communities that support the workers; appropriately resource the efforts. In short, organizing around sexual harassment violence is not the same as organizing around traditional economic issues: workers not getting paid, or lack of benefits, or even bad treatment on the job. Survivors of sexual harassment and violence know what they need—as the USWW's campaign slogan reminds us, "Janitors Know." The union should listen.

On a related note, unions within higher education that represent instructors, staff, and other professionals still have some work to do with regard to addressing sexual harassment. In her broad study of sexual harassment at universities, Sara Ahmed concluded that "we need a much fuller account of the role of unions in handling complaints made at universities," than she was able to document in her study.[58] She notes that she received many contrasting accounts of the role that unions play in handling complaints. Some people shared positive experiences, while others did not feel supported by the union because the union was perceived as having a "macho culture," or siding with the harasser, or being too close to management.

Hotel workers and their union, UNITE-HERE, have also been at the forefront of the ongoing struggle against sexual harassment. The power imbalance between male guests and housekeepers, who are often immigrants or women of color cleaning rooms in isolation, leaves the housekeepers vulnerable to abuse. The union has been campaigning to equip housekeepers and cleaners with panic buttons and has now secured local legislation in several cities that mandates panic buttons for all housekeepers, whether represented by a union or not.[59] The panic buttons are an important first step, and they bring real relief to the workers who toil in danger; whether or not they will lead to structural and cultural change is yet to be seen. Nonetheless, the efforts that led to securing local legislation were an essential step in worker self-empowerment. As Sara Lyons, one of the architects of the panic button campaign, explained,

We created a new space to come forward. This is a space where hospitality workers are invited to shed personal and collective self-doubt. We are invited to listen, to validate, and to back up one another. Imagine the ideas, solutions, connections, and transformations brought into the world when those marginalized or silenced are finally, heard![60]

Another promising practice comes from a more traditional, male-oriented union, the International Longshore and Warehouse Union (ILWU). Historically, that union maintained a provision in its contract that allowed the "son of an active deceased longshoreman" the right to join the union by "taking his father's union book"—a provision that remained until the mid-1970s, when a southern California female dock worker sued the union.[61] In 2001, the union negotiated a broad "no discrimination" clause with the Pacific Maritime Association in its Pacific Coast Longshore Contract that goes beyond what the law requires.[62]

The anti-discrimination clause is enforced through Section 13.2 of that instrument, which is an expedited grievance process. Complainants file a special form detailing the alleged act of discrimination, which goes to a rotating Area Arbitrator who determines whether the form states a claim under the anti-discrimination clause. If so, the Area Arbitrator schedules a hearing within 14 days. In the meantime, the Arbitrator has the power to issue a "separation order," in cases where the target and the accused work on the same shift—moving the accused to a different shift. If the hearing shows a violation of the clause, pay is mandatorily suspended for 30 days. The hearing officer has no latitude to reduce the penalty.

Complaints under this section are taken very seriously by the membership. According to Jim Monti, a former officer of ILWU Local 13 and now a consultant to the union who often serves as an Area Arbitrator, members often call each other out on inappropriate conduct. "You don't want to get 13.2d" is often heard on the docks.[63] Monti reports that in the decade that he has been working with the union, he has seen a significant shift in culture: moving away from masculinist horseplay to a more respectful environment. He attributes this change to the efforts of a former female general counsel who "insisted on negotiating the language and convinced leadership to devote substantial resources to training members on what Section 13.2 is all about."

A more recent sign of a shift in how unions deal with sexual harassment involves Local 802 of the American Federation of Musicians. In 2018, the New York Philharmonic fired the principal oboist, Liang Wang, and the associate principal trumpeter, Matthew Muckey, for unspecified misconduct.[64] The union grieved their discharges. The two were reinstated 19 months later after an arbitrator found that they had been terminated in violation of the collective bargaining agreement.[65]

The firings remained mysterious until April 2024, when Cara Kizer, a former member of the Philharmonic's brass section, shared details with *New York Magazine* of what Wang and Muckey did to her to warrant their dismissal in 2018.[66]

The details are horrendous. Ms. Kizer reported to the Denver Police Department while on tour with the Philharmonic in Colorado in 2010 that she had been sexually assaulted after spending an evening socializing with Wang and Muckey. She remembers drinking a glass of red wine that Wang brought her, and nothing else after that; she woke up the next morning in Muckey's bed, naked.

As she told *New York Magazine*, when she returned to her hotel room and prepared to take a shower, "she realized that a tampon that she had put in the previous day had been pushed so far into her vagina she had trouble removing it."[67] Every woman reading that sentence can feel the pain of what Ms. Kaizer must have gone through.

The police investigated the case, and after finding Muckey's DNA on Ms. Kizer's tampon, referred the case to the District Attorney's office for prosecution. The DA refused to prosecute.

According to *Vulture*, with no action from the DA's office, "the Philharmonic seemed to treat the issue as resolved. Muckey and Wang remained in the orchestra." Ms. Kaizer left New York.[68]

In early 2018, as #MeToo was gaining popularity, the Philharmonic returned to the allegations Ms. Kizer made against Muckey and Wang. It hired a retired federal judge who conducted a six-month investigation that determined that "the two men had engaged in misconduct warranting their termination."[69]

The union stepped in on behalf of the men. "The alleged conduct took place over 8 years prior, and much of the evidence appeared to be based on hearsay,"[70] the union explained. "Hearsay" is a legal term that is used colloquially to mean second-hand, unreliable information. In this case, the evidence included a DNA test, statements sworn under oath from the victim herself, and first-hand witnesses—far from hearsay.

The union took the case to arbitration. A well-known lawyer, Richard Bloch, served as the arbitrator. In 2020, he found in favor of the men. "Because 'sex acts are normally performed privately,' he wrote, 'the task of demonstrating assault charges, including those resulting from the refusal to take 'no' for an answer, can be difficult to prove."[71]

Within days of the *New York Magazine* article, the Philharmonic announced that Muckey and Wang would not take part in rehearsals or performances.[72] The men's future at the Philharmonic is not clear. Bloch's arbitration decision stands in the way of taking another look at the men's conduct.

But things have changed. This time, the union is not rushing to defend the men.

Sara Cutler, the president and executive director of the union who took office in 2023, told the *New York Times* that the decision to keep the men offstage for the time "are good first steps but they can't be the last." "As a woman, a musician and a new union president," she said, "I am horrified by what was in the story and we are committing the full resources of Local 802 to erase the culture of complicity that has raged at the N.Y. Philharmonic for too long."[73]

She also sent an update to the union's members:

I understand the allegations underlying this situation are triggering, horrifying, and even paralyzing to many of us. Many of us have suffered similar abuse or are close to someone who has. As a union and community, we should protect the most vulnerable—those who have been the targets of sexual abuse and violence. They deserve our unwavering support.[74]

The men are suing the union for failing to stand by them unequivocally, and the Philharmonic for breaching the collective bargaining agreement.[75] At a minimum, the case will give guidance to unions on how far they can go in terms of not using their resources to defend harassers. How far they *should* go is a different question—one that relies on changing the culture of the union with the support of the members. USWW and graduate students are clearing a path for unions to do just that.

6

The Global Response

To end harassment, we must unite our voices—locally and globally.

—Tarana Burke

Sexual harassment is a global problem affecting hundreds of millions of workers. Within ten days of the #MeToo hashtag going viral in the United States, it was trending in 85 different countries.[1] The hashtag sparked a worldwide conversation about sexual harassment: in France, survivors used #BalanceTonPorc ("snitch out your pig") to call out harassers; in Italy, #QuellaVoltaChe ("that time when") was widespread; in Spanish-speaking countries, survivors widely shared #YoTambien ("me too"); and in the Middle East and Africa, direct translations of "me too" went viral.[2] In the first month, more than 24 million people participated in the conversation on Facebook, commenting more than 77 million times.[3] Whether or not #MeToo will lead to structural changes is still up for debate. Meanwhile, survivors continue to speak their truth.

As late as 2022, no single global survey provided estimates of the frequency of sexual harassment around the world.[4] That year, the International Labour Organization (ILO)—the United Nations agency in charge of setting and monitoring global workers' rights—conducted a global survey of workers' own experiences of violence and harassment at work.[5] The survey revealed that sexual harassment is a recurrent and persistent problem, with more than 60 percent of survivors reporting that they have been harassed multiple times, and for the majority of them, that the last incident took place over the previous five years. It is also clear that the numbers are likely to be low: a little more than half (54 percent) of survivors reported that they shared their experiences only after having experienced more than one form of violence and harassment, and more likely with friends or family than reporting them through informal or formal channels.[6]

In addition, more than one-third of the world's countries do not have any laws prohibiting sexual harassment at work.[7] While laws do not guarantee that women will be free from harassment at work, the lack of legal protections leaves nearly 235 million working women vulnerable to harassment with no recourse.

There is no question that addressing sexual harassment must be a priority for unions around the world in policy and practice. Unions have been active on the policy front: they played a significant role in the development and adoption of ILO Convention 190—ratified in 2019—which is the first international legal framework explicitly addressing sexual harassment at work.[8] It is shocking that it took so long for global legal standards to acknowledge sexual harassment at work as a significant issue.

The Convention calls on governments to "adopt laws and regulations to define and prohibit violence and harassment in the world of work, including gender-based violence and harassment."[9] It also addresses workplace culture and high-lights the importance of mutual respect and human dignity in fostering safe and healthy workplaces. While most countries regulate sexual harassment at work through an anti-discrim-ination frame, the Convention takes a worker health and safety approach. Worker advocates on the drafting committee pushed this approach because it provides an alternative to the individualized victim, complaint-driven approach of anti-discrimination regimes to a "collective, structural and prevention-focused approach."[10] Treating sexual harassment at work as a serious workplace hazard also aligns well with what unions recognize as a core union value: the right to a safe job.[11]

As of February 2024, 38 countries have ratified the Convention, some with the help of trade unions. For example, in Uruguay, the first country to ratify Convention 190, unions, together with the Ministry of Labor, women's organizations, and the national trade union center, Pleanario Intersindical de Trabajadores-Convención Nacional de Trabajadores (PIT-CNT) ran a campaign that included workshops for members to understand that the Convention is a tool to grow worker power.[12]

Another promising example is the Trades Union Congress (TUC), England and Wales's main trade union federation, which has taken a serious approach to the issue. In 2021, the TUC General Council established an executive working group to support the TUC and affiliated unions in preventing, tackling, and effectively responding to sexual harassment within their organizations. The TUC's approach focuses on unions' roles as worker representatives and employers. This is a significant shift as it recognizes that unions are responsible for ending sexual harassment within the union movement. The working group's 2022 report notes that in 2018, the TUC updated its rules "to reflect this renewed focus on ending sexual harassment within our movement."[13] The new rule states:

It shall be a requirement of affiliation that an organisation has a clear commitment to promote equality for all and to

eliminate all forms of harassment, prejudice and unfair discrimination, both within its own structures and through all
its activities, including its own employment practices.

Notably, the TUC takes a preventative approach to the issue.[14]
Its member and leadership education efforts encourage
using climate assessments to identify risk factors. Its toolkit
recognizes that "the most prevalent risk factor for sexual
harassment is related to an institutional culture or climate,
specifically, a perceived tolerance for sexual harassment."[15]
Through the working group, the TUC has trained more than
50 senior leaders in the union movement in preventing sexual
harassment, piloted the training with several affiliates and
within its staff, and is now rolling this program out across the
movement.

As the TUC's Women's Policy Officer told me, the drive
for change came from below.[16] Female teachers and support
staff reported increased incidents of inappropriate sexual
comments and physical harassment by male colleagues and
male students and sought the unions' help. In the wake of
#MeToo, performing arts and entertainment unions became
increasingly vocal about the need for change. Research by the
Musicians' Union published in 2019 showed that almost half
of all workers in the industry faced sexual harassment.[17] As yet
another sign of positive change, the first female elected to head
the Musicians' Union (in 2022), Naomi Pohl, pledged to use
her tenure to stop the abuse, recognizing that "this is a culture
that needs to change."[18]

The TUC's shift also came at a time of disturbing public
reports of abuse by high-ranking elected leaders of TUC-
affiliated unions. One scandal involved the GMB union, one
of the largest trade unions in the United Kingdom. In 2020,

Tim Roache, the general secretary of the GMB, suddenly resigned in April, just five months after being re-elected to the position.[19] The union cited health issues as the reason for the resignation but quickly had to admit that it had received an anonymous letter that included several allegations about Roache and his senior staff. The letter, signed by "GMB sisters," asked that Roache be suspended immediately pending an investigation of a sexual assault that had been "discussed with concerning frequency" in the preceding weeks.[20] The letter also referred to a "longstanding culture of cover-up" and "a constant stream of rumours and stories within the union" about Roache's behavior. It claimed that senior GMB officials, as well as the TUC, the Labour Party, and several Members of Parliament (MPs) knew about the sexual assault. The letter also alleged that Roache created a "casting couch" culture in the union and accused senior staff of having "colluded many times in a cover-up of Tim Roache's sexist and aggressive behaviour towards women, while polishing their feminist credentials."[21]

The union appointed barrister Karon Monaghan to conduct an independent investigation. She issued a scathing report in September 2020, which concluded that "bullying, misogyny, cronyism and sexual harassment were 'endemic' within the union." The report includes themes that are eerily similar to the report of the investigation conducted in Washington, DC, of the conduct of J. David Cox, AFGE's former president. "The culture in the GMB is one of heavy drinking and late night socialising, salacious gossip and a lack of professionalism."

About sexual harassment, the report states:

> Examples of sexual harassment I heard about included touching hair, leering, commenting on body shape and clothes, placing hands around a woman's waist, staring at

a woman's breasts or "tits", propositioning young women, "sloppy kisses", "lip kisses", "sticking a tongue" in a woman's ear, touching of knees, bottoms and hips, hugs, and slapping of a backside. Sometimes sexual harassment is used as a form of bullying, with 54 examples given to me of men deliberately sexually harassing women in public to humiliate and embarrass them.

Monaghan further notes, "I have also heard of more serious sexual assaults. I was told by one witness that "it is simply expected that you'll have to suffer from being groped at events."

The report includes 27 recommendations to improve the union's culture. However, it also notes that "the reality is that the practices and culture of the GMB are so entrenched that a complete transformation is required. A fundamental shift in the GMB's culture and in the balance of power that exists within it, will be necessary if it is to become an inclusive and positive place in which to work and in which to participate as trade union members and activists."[22]

The union heeded at least one of the report's recommendations and established a task force to implement changes. However, it now seems clear that no fundamental shift in culture or practice has taken place within the GMB. Gary Smith was elected general GMB secretary in 2021, promising to fully implement Monaghan's recommendations. In March 2024, a female GMB employee released a recording in which Smith warns her about the consequences of filing a sexual harassment complaint. Initially, she attempted to lodge an internal complaint, but the GMB dismissed her concerns, claiming it was a personal matter and refused to investigate. She then filed a case with an employment tribunal. The recording captures Smith's reaction to her tribunal filing, where he cautions her about the potential repercussions of her actions, raising significant questions about the GMB's handling of sexual harassment complaints and the treatment of employees who come forward. As the *Herald* reported, Smith told her:

"You were in a shooting match."

"Once you get into a fight with a big organisation, we're going to come out swinging and we'll have better lawyers than you, and they'll be more expensive."

"That's just what happens. You put a gun on the table and we'll start shooting back."

"You start a shooting match, no greetin' once you've picked a fight in the manner that you did."

"There's a learning from there—don't get into that game, because everything then gets turned into something else. That's just life."

"The whole world is not about you and it's time to be very grown up about stuff."

He added: "You pulled the gun out. What did you want to happen?"

"You're going to start swinging guns about, people are going to start shooting back at you."[23]

Instead of taking responsibility for Smith's comments, the union told the *Daily Record* that it is considering legal action over the secret tapes. According to that publication, the union also emailed Labour MPs to say the comments were "highly misleading and conversations have been taken out of context."[24]

Long before its toxic culture came to light, the GMB implemented a code of conduct for members, activists, and employees and a zero-tolerance policy for harassment. These policies are worse than useless; they do nothing to prevent or remedy sexual harassment, and unions use them as cover when they are accused of harboring harassers and stoking a culture of abuse.

Another outrageous example of a union betraying its mission involves the Transportation Salaried Staffs' Association (TSSA). Claire Laycock, a former TSSA organizer, published a video with ReelNews in May 2022 where she shared her experiences of harassment as a TSSA staff member.[25] She exposed sexual harassment by the union's then-general secretary, Manuel Cortes, and other senior leaders and staff. The union adamantly denied Ms. Laylock's charges and tried to silence her by enforcing a non-disclosure agreement (NDA) she had signed when she left the union. Other women came forward, and the union was forced to commission an independent investigation, which Helena Kennedy KC conducted.

Baroness Kennedy issued her report in February 2023.[26] The inquiry uncovered a "mafia-like" culture of misogyny that condoned sexual harassment and violent behavior within the TSSA. The investigation revealed years of sexual assaults, unwanted touching, and manipulative behavior experienced by women working in the union. Specific instances include:

- Being so incapacitated from drinking the previous evening that they have failed to attend important work meetings the next day.
- "Doing business in the pub," "putting the union credit card behind the bar."

- Persistent attention to young women, violent, sexualised language ("you're off cockhunting are you?" calling people "cunts"), belittling women for their clothes, their general appearance, their education and seeking to undermine them and humiliate them ("no-one likes you," "you're useless").
- Staring—in a way that was experienced as highly intimidating, leering, inviting women for drinks and plying them with alcohol. Persistent insistence to women, particularly younger women, that they stay "for just one more drink" to the point where women cannot get home without help.
- Junior members of staff feeling the need to casually intervene or pretending to fall or trip to prevent pending incidents and protect colleagues ("he was about to put his hand on her backside so I pretended to trip" "I went and sat between them on the sofa.")
- "Specific examples I heard of non-consensual sexual behaviour included the sliding of a hand in between the upper thighs of a woman from behind, sliding a finger up and down the thigh of a young woman, squeezing breasts, repeatedly groping a woman from behind, whispering inappropriate suggestions ('if … I would fuck you …'), commenting on women's bodies or general appearance, asking women for a kiss and concentrated staring at a woman who had been harassed previously."
- Gaslighting and victim blaming of women who have tried to speak up ("they're too emotional" "they've got mental health problems" "they just became obsessed with x, y, z" "they're drinking too much and it's interfering with their medication" "this happened two years ago, you can't bring it up now").

- Trivialising women's experiences or assuming that they are lying.
- Belittling women by comparing women to each other in workplace environments, in terms of which woman is "more fun."
- Eye rolling or indicating "oh not this again," when people have tried to raise their concerns—a "boys will be boys" attitude.
- Using ostensibly legal language as a cover for inaction—"this was not corroborated," "there were no witnesses." The default position seems to be that women lie. The only proof of an incident having taken place, it seems, is for the incident to have been witnessed by the President, GS and his team.
- Using language about members that suggests disrespect or contempt, such as "write them [a member] a 'fuck off' letter"; "tell that person to take a running jump."
- Poor memory—it has been surprising to me how much cannot be recalled to mind by internal leadership—and yet how much is remembered, and consistently, by staff.

The report concluded that the internal leadership at the TSSA was "not fit for purpose." TSSA's president and treasurer resigned immediately after the report was issued. The TSSA's Executive Committee accepted the report and its recommendations, committing to implementing widespread change. Other than seeking the TUC's help, there are no public reports of what concrete steps the union has taken more than a year after the report.

A group of women and non-binary comrades have joined together under the banner of #MeTUWomen to end sexual harassment and bullying in the labor movement.[27] The group's

Twitter feed shows stories of resistance and constructive actions that trade union women and their allies are taking to make the labor movement align with the values it purports to advance: equity, dignity, fairness, and solidarity.[28] It is absolutely disgraceful that women have been forced to bear the burden of cleaning up the labor movement.

They may not have to do it alone. The TUC's actions hold promise. The ITUC has developed an impressive toolkit on Convention 190. Importantly, the toolkit includes a chapter titled, "Reforming our unions," which provides tools that unions can use to align their practices and policies with the mandate of Convention 190. The toolkit recognizes that

> Without equal and inclusive unions, we cannot effectively address violence and harassment in the world of work. But the inequality we see in society is unfortunately often seen in the union. Trade unions have historically been dominated by industrial workers—typically men. Still, today, the membership and leadership of trade unions is often dominated by men, and inequality is entrenched in the union culture, beliefs, and structures.[29]

Women unionists around the world face the challenge of working in a movement that prioritizes men and masculinist culture and continues to consider sexual harassment as a "personal" issue, not central to the core business of the unions.[30] As Linda Briskin and Patricia McDermott explain in their study of the Canadian labor movement, the areas within the labor movement that resist deeper change are:

> union complicity in the gendered segmentation of the labor market; union support for traditionalist ideologies about

women's work, breadwinner, and male-headed families, union resistance to broader-based bargaining; and patriarchal, bureaucratic, hierarchical, and often fundamentally anti-democratic union structures and practices which marginalize women inside unions.[31]

In South Africa, where sexual violence has been regarded as the highest in the world, unions follow the same playbook of their Western brothers.[32]

In 2013, a junior administrative assistant to the general secretary of COSATU, Zwelinzima Vavi, accused him of rape and sexual harassment.[33] Vavi explained during a television interview that he met the young woman "as one of the workers at SAA [South African Airways] and she was very efficient, very helpful and I was impressed." He later offered her a job at COSATU headquarters.

The young woman filed charges against him, and the federation investigated, but the investigation stopped when the young woman withdrew the charges. And, although Vavi lost his position as the general secretary of COSATU, this "sexual harassment saga" continues to have implications for COSATU and the South African labor movement.[34]

COSATU's 14th National Congress in 2022 was rocked by an allegation of rape and sexual harassment that took place on the first day of the Congress by a man described as a "popular leader." Women delegates rose from the floor to demand action. The federation issued a statement condemning the alleged rape.[35]

These allegations come within a long history of resistance by union leaders to address sexual harassment and sexual misconduct at a national conference. In 1989, women challenged COSATU leadership to adopt a resolution addressing sexual harassment in the workplace. Men strongly resisted. As Professor Malehoko Tshoaedi reports, "There were questions like 'why?', 'are we no longer supposed to touch you?'" Male delegates perceived the issue of sexual harassment as a private one, not worthy of unions' attention: "Women were told that the congress was concerned with 'serious' political issues which deserved the full attention of the congress."[36]

The federation finally adopted a code of conduct in 1994 as a result of allegations of serious misconduct by male unionists at one of the national congresses. According to Professor Tshoaedi's study of gender dynamics within COSATU, the code of conduct has been of limited value because it has done nothing to alter the underlying systems that allow harassment to exist in the first place.[37] Further, because the code of conduct is enforced by officials who are involved in sexist practices, most cases, especially those involving senior officials, are "pushed under the carpet."[38]

While unions around the world fall short in how they operate to address sexual harassment to the detriment of their staff, their members, and the institution, some global unions have prioritized the fight for gender justice and equality. The International Union of Food, Agricultural, Hotel, Restaurant, Catering, Tobacco, and Allied Workers' Associations (IUF) has been the leader in the fight against sexual harassment at work. IUF was formed in 1920 through the merger of several international trade union federations representing workers in the food, beverage, hospitality, agriculture, and related industries.[39] According to its website, in 2024, the union had 407 affiliated trade unions across 126 countries representing approximately 12 million workers.[40]

The global union began its work on sexual harassment in the 1980s, when the union's North American regional secretary, Joy Anne Grune, brought the issue to the governing body.[41] At that time, nearly half of the union's members were women. The union established women's committees in Asia and Africa, and in 1988, the Asia/Pacific Regional Committee adopted a policy on sexual harassment.[42] The union published a special issue of its newsletter, *Women at Work*, which included a handbook on how to deal with sexual harassment, "When I Say No, I Mean No."[43]

In 1987, the union's Executive Committee adopted a Memorandum on Equality, which, as Barbro Budin, the union's former gender equality officer explains, "made clear that sexual harassment is an issue of power, and not sexual interest." The union also took "a long-term and short-term approach" to the issue. The long-term approach sought to increase women's representation in leadership; at that time, the Executive Committee was composed of 29 men and two women, even though approximately half of the membership was female. IUF's directives now require that all its decision-making bodies include at least 40 percent women.

The increase in representation of women has made it easier to move the issue of sexual harassment forward. Importantly, the union has devoted time and resources to increasing the number of shop stewards and health and safety representatives, particularly in the agriculture sector. Past inspections by fair trade organizations didn't reveal the full extent of harassment because "women did not dare speak to them." The workers trusted their own shop stewards, and the union saw the incidents of harassment decrease. "It made a huge difference," according to Budin.

IUF took another important step by building on ILO Convention 184, which addresses safety and health in agriculture. In 2013, Sue Longley, the first woman to be elected general secretary of the IUF, led a team of unionists who negotiated a code of practice to help countries implement the convention. That code recognized that, "Sexual harassment is a hazard that lowers the quality of working life, jeopardizes the well-being of women and men, undermines gender equality and can have serious cost implications for firms and organizations."[44] The code also included a sample policy on sexual harassment.[45]

Rape, sexual assault, and harassment are alarmingly common for female farmworkers, enabled by vulnerabilities like migratory status, irregular employment or self-employment, language barriers, and working in isolation. As the journalist Bernice Yeung explained in relation to the documentary she helped produce, *Rape in the Fields*, a "supervisor with a paycheck or a job to handout is in a position where he can extract just about anything from his workers."[46]

One of the main points of contention during the discussions in Convention 184 was about separate toilets for men and women. The employers argued that it would be very costly and complicated to establish separate sanitation facilities; "the problem is that a lot of assaults took place when women went to the toilet because they couldn't close the door," and the same problem existed with regard to changing rooms.[47] The employers won.[48]

The language in the code of practice was instrumental in moving the issue forward institutionally. One of the IUF's strategies since its inception was to negotiate global framework agreements with multinational corporations. Through these agreements, multinational corporation agree to abide by the ILO's core conventions: freedom of association, collective bargaining, child labor, and forced labor.

The language in the code of practice carved a path for the IUF and the Coordinating Body of Latin American Banana

Workers' Unions (COLSIBA) to negotiate an appendix to their framework agreement with the banana company Chiquita in 2013, establishing a joint understanding on sexual harassment.[49] IUF has now negotiated international agreements to address sexual harassment with seven global corporations that cover workers in 54 countries.

I am certain that there are stories of unions taking bold and innovative steps to address sexual harassment that I have not captioned here. I am more removed from the global aspects of this work than I am from the story of the United States. The bigger story would not be complete without global reflections. My hope is that this chapter serves as an entry point for a larger, more promising story.

I should also note that this chapter has focused on traditional trade unions. Emerging unions and those operating in sectors not traditionally represented by trade unions are doing inspiring work, which I cover in the next chapter, as recommendations for traditional unions.

7
Change Is Essential

Change is the law of life, and those who look only to the past
or present are certain to miss the future.

—John F. Kennedy

The labor movement should stop enabling sexual harassment.
Unions should stop defending harassers and ignoring their
own role in promoting cultures that encourage the exploitation of women. The hyper-masculine culture that continues
to define the labor movement betrays both its values of solidarity, equity, justice, fairness, and dignity and the women it
purports to protect. It also keeps the movement from growing,
leaving it open to the very critiques that employers use when
trying to bust a union.

The stories told in these pages of women who sought help
from their unions only to be turned away, or worse, further
abused, reflect more than a generation of union women's
pain, anger, and betrayal. Roxanne's shock at receiving lewd
texts from her union representative while working at a union
echoes Sara's feelings of betrayal as the union she loved turned
its back on her. The women in these pages share the want, pain,
and degradation of working under the norms of toxic masculinity. Rocky fared no better early in his union path. To all of
them, the union did not mean justice, equity, or solidarity.

This is not to say that no unions have made visible cultural
shifts. Union janitors in Los Angeles changed the culture of
their union by taking a hard look inside, deciding that the

macho culture that secretly guided the experiences of staff and members needed to change—and changing that culture. The New York Musicians' Union's new leadership also offers hope in erasing the culture of complicity that has raged within the U.S. labor movement.

Where does change begin? Unions have a dual identity that makes them uniquely able to shatter sexist norms. On the one hand, unions are collective bargaining agents, where they battle capital to institutionalize the gains that workers make on the ground. On the other hand, unions are employers and often sit at the bargaining table across from their own employees, who are also seeking equity and safety within the union.

The following are some ideas of how unions can change course and shift workplace culture to one that values diversity, inclusion, dignity, and respect, as well as a climate that puts these values into action.

RECONCEPTUALIZE SEXUAL HARASSMENT AND RECOGNIZE IT AS A CORE UNION ISSUE

First, unions must acknowledge that they have a responsibility to eradicate sexual harassment. Unions are much more comfortable simply pointing the finger at the employer. The American Federation of State, County and Municipal Employees' (AFSCME) secretary-treasurer, Elissa McBride, hosted an online conversation in the first months of #MeToo where the issue of who is responsible for harassment came up repeatedly, almost as if it were the central theme. At one point, McBride interrupted a speaker discussing workplace dynamics: "In fact, it is the law; it is management's responsibility to create a harassment-free workplace. Our responsibility as advocates is to encourage, pressure, and assist, but the responsibility lies with management. I think it's really important we're clear about that."[1] The union reinforces that idea on its website, where it tells its members: "If you observe harassment in the workplace, whether or not the victim complains, make efforts to stop it and put management on notice of the harassment; it is the employer's responsibility to provide a harassment-free environment."[2] AFSCME is not alone. Thomas Carpenter, the general counsel of Actor's Equity, the union of theatrical performers, told a reporter, "It's hard to change the culture of the workplace, but it's the employer's responsibility to do that," which amounts to an abdication of centuries of trade unionism.[3]

Of course, employers have an obligation to provide a safe workplace, but that in no way should diminish the union's own responsibility to address and prevent sexual harassment. The collective bargaining process gives workers a voice in setting the terms and conditions of their employment. That means that unions bargain all types of policies, including health and safety protocols, breaks, schedules, smoking policies, drug testing, and more. In fact, U.S. labor law imposes a mutual obligation on the employer and the union to negotiate in good faith over wages, hours, and other terms and conditions of employment. Sexual harassment policies are a mandatory subject of bargaining, which means that if the employer refuses to bargain over those policies after the union puts that topic on the bargaining agenda, the employer would violate the law. Similarly, the employer acts unlawfully if it unilaterally implements or changes a sexual harassment policy. The fact that unions don't even attempt to bargain those policies reflects a dereliction of responsibility—often to its detriment. As Professor Marion Crain explains:

Labor's voice is silenced in rooms where anti-sexual harassment policies are created. All workers suffer as a result: unionized workers are deprived of a representative on an issue fundamental to safe and productive workplaces, and nonunion workers learn to see unions as largely irrelevant in the struggle to eradicate discrimination at work—a strategic mistake in an increasingly diverse labor force.

Another problem is that too often, unions view sexual harassment through a sexual desire-dominance paradigm that involves sexualized conduct by a supervisor or manager with a person over whom he wields power, what Professor Vicki Schultz describes as the "top-down, male-female, sexual come-on image of harassment."[4]

That perception fits comfortably within the preferred blame-the-boss narrative, leaving the union with little responsibility yet disingenuously promoting unionization as the solution. The AFL-CIO's guidance on the topic explains, "[g]iven that sexual harassment is an abuse of power, typically by a male manager against female subordinates, having a union and collective voice strengthens a worker's ability to stop [the] harassment. A woman facing sexual harassment is not alone."[5]

That preconception is wrong: most studies show that abuse of power by a manager over subordinates accounts for less than 4 percent of workplace sexual harassment. In fact, more than 60 percent of harassment is committed by coworkers—another aspect of the problem that unions don't want to face. During the AFSMCE online conversation, a male member asked, "What do we do when the accused and the accuser are both members of your local? Where do we find the balance to support both of them?" An appropriate answer to that question requires understanding a union's legal duty to its members, which is to act in a manner that is not "arbitrary, discriminatory or in bad faith." As we saw in Chapter 4, if a harasser is disciplined and files a grievance, the union has to investigate the grievance, but as one court made clear, "the union has no duty to represent members for discipline they incurred for engaging in sexually or racially harassing conduct."[6] Instead of outlining the union's duty in these circumstances, Liz Shuler, the AFL-CIO's current president, gave a rambling, confusing explanation that underscores the lack of understanding of this basic, fundamental union principle:

I think it is a tricky situation but we face it quite often ... not just with sexual harassment but with any kind of workplace incident. Say there's a fight that breaks out in the workplace, or [another situation where] there are two members involved ... who represents whom? I guess the quick answer is that we do represent both members and that every member is entitled to a fair process and a due process and making sure that the workplace procedures are followed. As we said at the top ... the employer is actually technically responsible ... legally responsible. So, making sure that the employer's rules are followed, I think, is really our union role to begin with and that ... we have ... the complaint procedures in place, we have the investigation steps outlined, we [are] making sure that we're really listening and taking in the information, making sure that discipline is appropriate, making sure there's no retaliation ... and making that clear ... so the Union can be a helpful voice in ensuring that those processes are followed and that we're really advocating and, as I said, making sure we're taking seriously these complaints ...[7]

The sex-dominance paradigm that unions prefer also places too much emphasis on sex, ignoring the fact that sexual harassment is a means for men to claim work as masculine turf, often with no reference to sex or sexual innuendo. Lois Jenson discovered this hard truth on the first day she and her sisters entered the iron ore mine in northern Minnesota. A male coworker expressed his opposition to their presence in the mine in no uncertain terms: "You fucking women don't belong here. If you knew what was good for you, you'd go home where you belong."[8] Men often don't have to say anything to harass women successfully: in construction, men hide women's tools or assign them to dangerous tasks without proper safety equipment. A tradeswoman in New York reported "being pinched, pushed, put on coffee duty, made to dangle from skyscraper pillars without safety equipment, ranted at, and fired repeatedly for no reason."[9] That sort of behavior exists in other male-dominated workplaces as well. In a hospital, male surgical residents went so far as to falsify a patient's medical records to make it appear that their female colleague had made an error. Harassment in these settings is designed to ensure women feel unwelcome, unfit, and unable to do the job.[10]

Rather than advance conceptions of harassment that are, at best, outdated, unions should follow the lead of social scientists and legal scholars, who view sexual harassment as composed of three distinct but related categories of behavior: sexual coercion, unwanted sexual attention, and gender harassment. These categories give a much better sense of the types of behavior that constitute harassment and, more importantly, how victims experience the harassment. Given that gender harassment is by far the most common type of sexual harassment, unions should be focusing on addressing behaviors that fall under that category.

Gender harassment refers to "a broad range of verbal and nonverbal behaviors not aimed at sexual cooperation, but that convey insulting, hostile, and degrading attitudes about" members of one gender. Examples include comments about women not belonging in the workplace, crude jokes, display of naked women and pornography, use of language such as "bitch," or "slut," and phrases such as "don't be a pussy"—the types of behaviors that women in auto plants, on construction sites, and in other male-dominated union shops experience daily.[11] Roxanne's experience while doing clerical work for the Pennsylvania AFL-CIO is a clear example of this type of harassment. In the two years she worked at the union-related organization, she watched her bosses push all of her female coworkers to tears. "Frank would fly off the handle for no reason and yell and pound his fist, but never at the men," she told me. Rick repeatedly told her that women "are only good for clerical work" and constantly reminded her that if he fired her, she would never find work in the area again.[12] That behavior should never be tolerated, especially not by workers' rights organizations.

FOCUS ON CULTURE

Organizational culture is the single most important factor in determining whether sexual harassment is likely to occur.[13] Cultures reflect the norms and values of those in leadership; they influence the allocation of resources and determine who and what behaviors are valued. Workplace culture is "how we behave when no one's watching." If workers perceive the workplace culture to be permissive of sexual harassment, employees are at high risk of suffering sexual harassment. We've explored the sexist culture that persists within the labor movement—from iconography to outrageous practices like the Union Sportsmen Alliance fundraisers held at AFL-CIO headquarters where models in micro mini-skirts and 5-inch heels serve as hostesses, despite protests from the staff about the event's degrading and sexist nature.

Macho culture goes beyond sexism: it also includes aggressive, sometimes violent behavior that is meant to carve out turf. Roxanne and the other women at the Pennsylvania AFL-CIO are witnesses to that behavior. Given those cultures, it is no surprise that unions don't see or take seriously their responsibility in creating and maintaining harassment-free workplaces.

Climate assessment surveys would help unions understand their culture, identify areas needing attention, and track culture change over time. Social scientists have developed various methods of measuring the prevalence of sexual harassment that can help unions in this regard. For example, one way of assessing organizational tolerance for sexual harassment is by analyzing three factors: (1) the perceived risk to targets for complaining, (2) the perceived lack of sanctions against offenders, and (3) the perception that complaints will not be taken seriously. Surveys can also measure sexist social norms and men's attitudes about women—factors that contribute to cultures that tolerate harassment. The TUC has developed a culture checklist that all unions could modify to meet their needs.

A note of caution: in sectors where sexual harassment is endemic, workers may not conceptualize their experiences as sexual harassment. The Restaurant Opportunities Center documented this phenomenon in its study of the restaurant industry in 2014, where more than 80 percent of servers experience habitual harassment.[14] Substantial worker education should precede such surveys.

The information from these surveys can be used for training, coaching, mentoring, and guiding collective bargaining.

Unions should use their power at the bargaining table to require employers to conduct those surveys regularly and to monitor progress.

Acting together, unions would significantly impact modeling culture and behavior change. With the consent of the majority of unions, the AFL-CIO could require all unions to conduct climate assessment surveys annually and make those reports public. In 2005, the AFL-CIO Convention adopted a sweeping resolution on improving diversity in labor movement leadership. That resolution required "national unions to report annually on the representation of women and people of color in their membership as well as in staff and elected leadership positions at all levels." The added requirement of making the information accessible to the public would show members, workers who are not yet in unions, and labor movement observers that the commitment to change is real.[15]

At the international level, the International Trade Union Confederation (ITUC) could require that national federations report on the culture in their countries annually, thereby encouraging transparency and rewarding those unions that engage in the complex change process.

INTEGRATE NEW PARADIGMS INTO LABOR EDUCATION AND TRAINING

Women have been a focus of labor education efforts for decades.[16] Various university labor education programs host women's summer schools, bringing rank-and-file members together with union staff, elected officials, and academics. The agenda typically includes public speaking, grievance handling, labor history, and internal organizing.[17] The Women's Institute for Leadership Development (WILD) is one internal labor education effort tailored to women's needs. A group of union women founded WILD in 1986 in Massachusetts to "strengthen women's influence in the labor movement by increasing the number and diversity of women leaders, and providing them with tools to be effective organizers in their unions and organizations."[18] WILD also describes its mission as "building awareness of and stimulating debate about issues of racism, sexism, class, homophobia and other issues of oppression within unions and the larger labor movement." Thousands of women have gone through these programs, built relationships that undoubtedly helped them in their careers, and forged lifelong friendships.

In terms of dismantling the structures of sexual harassment, however, these programs fall short. They do an excellent job of helping women develop much-needed coping strategies. In one common and beloved exercise, instructors hand out pieces of paper with images of bricks. Women are asked to write down the challenges they face in their jobs and as members or union leaders—one challenge per "brick." Participants then build a wall with their bricks at the front of the classroom—a concrete image of women's daily struggles. Instructors then distribute paper cut-outs of feet, and ask the participants to write down how they handle the challenges reflected on the bricks. The students then place their paper feet on the wall, reassuring each other that overcoming those challenges is possible. This exercise acts as a pressure-release valve for many women. It does not, however, focus on smashing the wall, which is where unionists' focus should be.

A more interesting exercise would be to depict a crane and wrecking ball next to the wall and ask the students to fuel the equipment with ideas.

The Los Angeles janitors' union's ground-breaking *promotora* program is an example of what labor education around the issue of sexual harassment should be: developed and led by workers, mandated across the industry, and paid for by employers. The program has transformed the lives of *promotoras*. At a labor education conference in 2018, an elderly *promotora*, Anabela, described her journey, which led her to an awakening. "I had to admit that I was living in a macho culture," she told conference participants. She cleaned office buildings at least eight hours a day and was responsible for cleaning the house, cooking, and even ironing her grandchildren's clothes. She did this without a thought, she explained, "until one day I asked myself, 'Why should I be doing all of this when I already work harder than anyone in this house?'" She talked to her family about the gendered roles that defined their households, and each slowly began to adapt to a new reality where each was responsible for duties that previously belonged only to the *promotora*. When Anabela saw that she could change the culture at home, she knew she could do the same on the job. Anabela's journey mirrors the journey of more than a hundred women who have gone through the *promotora* program and are now changing gendered norms at home and on the job. This program is an example of what could be fueling the wrecking ball.

The union also created a program for men, *compadres* (comrades), which serves as a space where men explore masculinity and their roles—as individuals and as a collective—in perpetuating cultures of harassment, which is another area that needs much more attention.[19]

Union education efforts must also address internal union cultures. Efforts in the United States need to be improved in this regard. The AFL-CIO's culture change curriculum, "Culture Change Training: Addressing Unwanted Behavior in Our Movement," doesn't even mention assessing internal union culture structurally.[20] Instead, it promotes focusing on individual behaviors and aligning those with union values— reminiscent of employer diversity, equity, and inclusion efforts. Its only guidance is "taking personal responsibility to address or intervene." In other words, the AFL-CIO recommends bystander intervention as the answer to the toxic, abusive union culture that courses through the U.S. labor movement. Remember that when Roxanne reached out to Liz Shuler for help, rather than practice "bystander intervention," Shuler had a lawyer respond, claiming that the AFL-CIO was not responsible for what happened.

The practice scenarios in the curriculum are deficient. In one, a local labor leader sends an email congratulating Jamal, one of two Black staff members, for the work of the only other Black staff member, Jerome. No one corrects this mistake. "Is this a problem?" the curriculum asks, and if so, how do you intervene?

In the other, Lin, a young Asian American organizer, makes a suggestion at a meeting, and everyone ignores her. Then Joel, the political director, makes the very same suggestion, and people congratulate him for his innovative solution. "Lin appears unfazed," students are told before they are asked, "Is this a problem?" And if so, how do you intervene?

These are not unrealistic examples of what union staff constantly go through. In my day, we called the latter the "I just said that" problem. They are both symptoms of a much larger problem: racism and misogyny baked into the institution. Individual interventions will not change the structures, especially when the institution punishes those challenging the norms.

The TUC and ITUC offer suggestions on internal structural change in their education materials, which is a positive step. The TUC's approach is subtle: It first recognizes that unions have responsibilities as employers for creating harassment-free workplaces. Then, it provides tools for unions as employers to do just that—baby steps.

The ITUC's training materials are more direct, providing various suggestions for unions to ensure that "our own organisations and operations are free from violence and harassment." Those include risk assessments (i.e., climate assessments), internal policies and procedures for unions as model employers, practical training, integrating gender-responsive approaches into collective bargaining, amending constitutions and other governance documents to ensure that such an approach is integrated into all decision-making structures, and more.

One cautionary note on internal union codes of conduct: ITUC's materials refer to the AFL-CIO's code of conduct as a model. Codes of conduct (or toolkits) alone do nothing to change culture. Most, if not all, of the unions that enabled the abuse of their staff and members highlighted in this book had such a code of conduct. The enforcement of those codes is critical, and so far, there is no evidence that unions enforce codes of conduct meaningfully. I'll share an anecdote to bring home the point: in 2019, a young woman contacted me about her experience at the Denver Area Labor Federation, AFL-CIO. She told me that representatives of the building trades were on stage making disparaging comments about climate change activists. She rose to address those comments and said that she did not appreciate old white men dictating the future of the planet and the labor movement—or words to that effect. Less than a month later, she received a letter from Josh Downey, the president of the Labor Federation, which states:

> I am writing in regard to an incident that occurred on August 22, 2019, at the Denver Area Labor Federation (DALF) Delegate meeting. During the course of regular business, you rose to address the body and referred to some delegates as "old white men." After further investigation, it is the opinion of the DALF Ethics Committee and the DALF Executive Board that this statement was in violation of the DALF Code of Conduct and Anti-Discrimination and Anti-Harassment Policy.[21]

The letter asks the young woman to "treat all fellow attendees with respect and refrain from inflammatory and disparaging language in the future." It continued, "We would also encourage you to meet with the individual complainants to aid in the fence mending process," and warned that further violations of the code "will result in further disciplinary action."

I read this letter as retaliatory and a violation of the code of conduct. Clearly, the code of conduct was not meant to protect old white men nor to silence dissent. I sent the letter to the national AFL-CIO and heard nothing. Enforcement matters.

CHANGE HOW THEY DISCHARGE THEIR COLLECTIVE BARGAINING DUTIES

Unions should stop unquestioningly defending harassers at the expense of survivors—whether the harasser is a leader, a member, or a brilliant staff person. There's no doubt that holding people accountable is difficult, especially when those people have been loyal trade unionists. But as the late-night television host Stephen Colbert said when his mentor, the former head of CBS, Les Moonves, was accused of sexual harassment and abuse, "Everybody believes in accountability until it's their guy. And make no mistake, Les Moonves is my guy. But accountability is meaningless unless it's for everybody. Whether it's the leader of the network or the leader of the free world."[22]

Unions know that their obligation to members—the duty of fair representation—gives them tremendous leniency in handling grievances; the case books are full of instances where unions refused to proceed with a grievance, the grievant complained, and the legal authority sided with the union. Hiding behind that thin legal responsibility as justification for taking harassers' cases to arbitration when the accusations are true tells survivors what the patriarchy has always told women: you are a liar. We believe the guy.

Instead, unions should take the approach of the Los Angeles janitors' union, which negotiated contractual language that specifies that when the union is satisfied that the employer's investigation is thorough, it will not question the findings. In other words, the union exercises its responsibility to protect workers by ensuring that the employer's investigation is thorough and fair and stands with the victim instead of simply pointing her in the direction of the employer. This simple change in approach signals to victims of harassment and women in general that the union is on their side.

In terms of the level of discipline that harassers receive, unions should focus on the harm suffered by the victims and adopt practices that alleviate that harm while at the same time treating the harasser fairly. Most women who suffer sexual harassment are not interested in filing grievances or complaints, and many don't necessarily want the harasser to be fired; they simply want the harassment to stop. Informal resolution mechanisms that address the offensive conduct and give the victim a voice would complement grievance processes or, in some cases, provide an alternative.

Consider the case of two young women who graduated from a fire academy in Rhode Island in early 2020.[23] We'll call them Andrea and Daniela. They are the only two women who have ever worked in the brigade, which consists of 107 firefighters. Andrea received a Facebook message from someone she didn't know, congratulating her on being in the Academy. A few months later, a senior firefighter, Greg, approached her at the scene of a fire and told her that he was the person who had sent her the message; then, he said, "this is kind of awkward because I have a girlfriend now but if you need anything, I'm here." She didn't know what to make of this. Greg was a lieutenant with 32 years in the brigade.

Greg's messages and texts increased, mainly in the evening. In one, he told her that he adored her because she's gay. In another, he told her that she would come home one day, and "you and your wife will be sipping bloody Mary's. Xoxoxo." He also texted, "ick, ick, ick, women are beautiful from the belly button up," and "Hey babe, can I call you that?"

Andrea later testified that she was "creeped out" by the texts, which became more and more bizarre. He asked her to buy drugs for him, telling her, "You're my connection to the good stuff, so don't disappoint." Andrea immediately responded, "Omg, no. I don't do that," but Greg pressed on, "Come on. Just recreational fun here and there … BTW, none of this has any impact on us," and "I usually buy here and there from another lesbian friend, but her stuff is shit."

Daniela graduated from the Academy a year before Andrea. Greg also sent her a Facebook message while she was at the Academy. He sent her messages inviting her to socialize. During a social event at a bar, Greg tried to kiss Daniela on the mouth, but her boyfriend (another firefighter) intervened. He continued to send her strange messages. He told her he had "come out" as bisexual and that he wanted to do his own makeup one day. He told her that "he would like to do prostitution sometime and asked her what type of lip gloss she would use for oral sex." He also sent her messages about buying cocaine.

Daniela's boyfriend reported Greg. The Department conducted an investigation, which revealed his conduct towards Andrea, and he was fired. The union stepped in.

In defending Greg, the union argued that although Greg initiated the messages, both women "responded to his messages, they befriended him on Facebook, and at no time did they ever block his texts or unfriend him on Facebook." Therefore, the union argued, "It was not unreasonable for Grievant [Greg] to think that his texts and messages were considered friendly and were not considered by either [woman] to be offensive or abusive."

Andrea was in her probationary period during this time, which meant that she could be fired for any reason; her contractual provisions had not yet kicked in. A coworker testified at the arbitration hearing that Andrea was "visibly upset" by the messages. Andrea testified that since Greg was a superior, "and she was still a probationary firefighter, she did not want to block his text messages as he would know that she had blocked his messages, and she wanted to keep the peace between them." She also testified that "she felt uncomfortable working with him as a result of his text messages, but that she did not really know whom to go to, to have him stop."

The union framed the grievance as a sexual harassment case, and the arbitrator applied anti-discrimination law. He found that Greg's actions "went way beyond an employee-supervisor relationship," but amounted to "poor judgment," not sexual harassment. He concluded: "no evidence that Grievant's conduct impacted [Andrea or Daniela's] employment in any way." The text messages were "annoying and bothersome," and "as time passed, his messages to [Andrea and Daniela] were requests for help from a troubled man," he found.

The union presented Greg in a very compassionate light: he was "dealing with emotional issues related to the death of the prior president of the union and having responded to the suicide of a young woman during a work call." Also, he was "drinking heavily during the time period." The arbitrator showed similar compassion: "he sought injury leave for what he believed was post-traumatic stress having responded to suicide during a response," and the death of the former union president. Greg's conduct was not "maliciously motivated." He "sought out the two female firefights because ... he was looking for friends that he assumed would identify and be sympathetic with him as a gay or bi-sexual firefighter." The arbitrator continued, "Although Grievant testified that he had used cocaine and was drinking heavily at that time, there is no evidence that his responsibilities at the firehouse were in any way compromised or that he was ever unable to perform his duties."

The women were invisible, other than as the recipients of Greg's "poor judgment." The arbitrator showed no compassion or concern for the women. The employer was the only entity

that raised the power imbalance; the women were probationary firefighters, and Greg was a seasoned veteran. Nor is there
any recognition that these women were the very first to join
the brigade. In his defense, the union argued that Greg had
never sent texts like these to anyone in the past. One would
not know that the union represented the women.

This case underscores the need for the union to adopt a definition of sexual harassment that better aligns with women's
experiences on the job. It also highlights the need for a way to
stop the harassment—not through a grievance or other legalistic process. As Andrea explained, all she wanted was for the
harassment to stop.

Restorative justice mechanisms are worth exploring.
Restorative justice mechanisms are premised on the wrong-
doer accepting responsibility and engaging with the victim
to address the harm. Outcomes are not punitive. The process
offers a much broader range of remedies, from asking for an
apology to conducting a forum to discuss what happened to
anything in between.[24]

Restorative justice practices have been used in schools,
hospitals, communities, and criminal justice systems, slowly
making their way into workplaces. They hold great promise in
the sphere of sexual harassment because they give the victim
a voice throughout the process, which helps her deal with
the confusion and mental anguish that trauma vests. One of
the most harmful aspects of how unions and the legal system
handle complaints is that they keep information secret from
the victim. From the standpoint of a survivor, the process is
a dark gauntlet. It usually consists of an investigation (where
those interviewed are instructed not to talk to anyone), a
report that management or the union do not share with the
victim, and an outcome most often shared with the victim as

a one-sentence conclusion, with no explanation. This system leaves the survivors feeling alone, confused, and frequently alienated from their peers.

A restorative justice process in the workplace might look like this: first, the facilitator spends time with the survivor and the harasser separately, assessing the extent of the harm and the harasser's willingness to accept responsibility for his actions. The facilitator then convenes a meeting called a "circle," a conversation that includes the survivor, people who the survivor needs for support, and the harasser. The conversation centers the victim by focusing on the harm she suffered and her path to healing. Those in the circle decide the outcomes. Nothing is predetermined or out of bounds.

A note of caution: If the survivor does not want to engage in the process or the harasser is not ready to accept responsibility, the process cannot go forward. This is an important point because many people misunderstand the goal of restorative justice, which is to heal a collective harm. It is not to allow perpetrators to escape punishment or to treat harassers more kindly. The process belongs to those who are harmed, not to the harassers. I do not make this point for theoretical purposes. In the course of my conflict resolution work for a political organization, I have encountered several men accused of harassment who demand restorative justice. Not surprisingly, these men are unable to articulate the harm they caused, much less accept responsibility for their behavior. They are shocked when I turn them away, forcing them into a traditional grievance process.

Unions can easily include these restorative justice practices in a collective bargaining agreement. After all, grievance processes are the most common feature of such agreements, and restorative practices are a wonderful complement to those existing processes.

DEVELOP A MORE INCLUSIVE
AND BROADER LABOR FEMINISM

Women have played a complex and paradoxical role in the labor movement, involving struggle—especially at the grassroots level—and complicity in preserving patriarchal structures and economistic agendas. For example, when women unionists formed the Coalition for Labor Union Women (CLUW) in 1974 as a constituency group of the AFL-CIO, they sought to develop a working women's agenda without attacking the male labor establishment. They wanted to win support from and gain credibility within the official labor leadership. Women believed that it was not in their interest to challenge the patriarchy or sexism within labor's own ranks as it would subject them to accusations of disloyalty and engender men's wrath. Instead, they focused on economic issues.[25]

That economistic approach to labor feminism has resulted in an "add women of color and stir" model, which universalizes the experiences of white women, or adds statistics about the hyper-exploitation of non-cis white women to the narrative. If the labor movement were shaped by the experiences of non-white women, the institution would look beyond economic issues and focus on the multiple factors that shape workers' lives, which would operate to the benefit of all women.

The time has come for union women to reconsider past choices and to mold a feminism that aligns with the reality of today's working women. That means taking on internal sexism, and confronting the embedded divide among white women and women of color that continues to define working women's lives. As Audre Lorde cautioned long ago,

> For the master's tools will never dismantle the master's house. They may allow us temporarily to beat him at his own game, but they will never enable us to bring about genuine change. And this fact is only threatening to those women who still define the master's house as their only source of support.[26]

MODEL EMPLOYER BEHAVIOR

As employers, unions have a unique opportunity to model proper employer behavior by, for example, transparently assessing their own organizational climates, bargaining broad sexual harassment provisions in their staff union contracts, and allocating resources to anti-harassment efforts. While statements from leaders are important, history teaches us that they are not nearly enough. The British TUC took an important step, small as it may be, in recognizing that within its role as an employer, it could influence unions to do the same and move the institution to make the necessary structural change.

Importantly, unions should lead the way in holding insiders accountable for sexual harassment. Unions should not offer aid and comfort to sexual harassers, no matter how smart, strategic, or close to leadership the harasser happens to be.

It remains to be seen whether the labor movement will take responsibility for its own internal harassment problems in a meaningful way. As we saw in these pages, the labor movement's internal #MeToo reckoning lost steam within a year of the various exposés of powerful men, including labor leaders. The AFL-CIO never issued its much-touted report on sexual harassment. The SEIU's Blue Ribbon Commission on Sexual

Harassment faded away with no findings, no proposed changes or programs. Liz Shuler's adulation of Roxanne's abusive boss in April 2022, as an "incredible leader," despite knowing how he treated women was a depressing sign.

But it's not too late. The labor movement can learn from Oxfam, a global organization that faced an internal sexual harassment problem, and took immediate steps to address the problem, both internally and for the international aid community in which it functions. In addition to setting up an independent commission, the organization developed a plan along various streams of work, providing a framework for how it will improve its transparency, accountability, policies, practices, and culture; increase investment into safeguarding and training; work with other non-governmental organizations (NGOs); and reform its recruitment and vetting processes. The plan is prominent on Oxfam's web page, which also tracks the effort's progress and promises updates every six months.[27] One major accomplishment is a pledge, signed by 118 heads of international aid organizations, which includes taking steps to ensure perpetrators cannot be re-employed by other members of the international aid community.

Organizational accountability is not about singling out bad actors; it is an essential element of eradicating sexual harassment. The labor movement has a higher moral duty to ensure that women who dedicate their time, energy, and commitment to the movement are able to work safely and with dignity, free from sexual harassment.

STOP USING NON-DISCLOSURE AGREEMENTS (NDAs)

NDAs perpetuate sexual harassment by effectively silencing survivors and shielding perpetrators from accountability.

These legal contracts prohibit survivors from speaking about their experiences, which not only prevents them from seeking support and healing but also allows abusers to continue their harmful behavior unchecked.[28] On a systemic level, NDAs contribute to broader issues surrounding sexual harassment by perpetuating power imbalances and hindering efforts to change workplace cultures.

The law is starting to recognize the harmful effects of NDAs. Several U.S. states have restricted NDAs in cases of sexual harassment or discrimination.[29] California led the way in 2018 by prohibiting NDAs in settlements involving sexual assault, harassment, or sex discrimination. In 2023, the National Labor Relations Board banned the use of NDAs in severance agreements on the grounds that such agreements prevent workers from sharing information about workplace conditions, which violates the National Labor Relations Act.[30]

Several unions have taken strong stances against NDAs in cases of workplace harassment and discrimination. The Daily Beast Union set a new standard in the media industry by successfully negotiating a contract that bans NDAs in cases of both harassment and discrimination. Similarly, the New Yorker Union also secured a ban on NDAs in cases of harassment and discrimination in their first union contract.[31]

Yet, as employers, unions continue to use NDAs extensively. I have spoken to tens of women who worked in unions over the past five years who want to share their stories of harassment but are bound to silence by a union-imposed NDA. The situation is no different in the United Kingdom, where the GMB called for a ban on NDAs at its 2023 congress, particularly around cases of sexual harassment and discrimination. A March 2024 investigation by the *Sunday Mail* found at least three cases where female employees have been asked to sign

NDAs as part of agreements to settle employment disputes including sex discrimination, harassment, and bullying.[32]

The AFL-CIO should implement a federation-wide ban on the use of NDAs by its affiliated unions, even if individual unions are reluctant to do so voluntarily. A more transformative approach would be to accompany the ban on NDAs with a policy releasing all survivors from their NDAs, and broadly publicize that policy. These policies would align union practices with the protections they advocate for their members and send a powerful message of support to survivors of workplace harassment.

LOOK FOR INSPIRATION OUTSIDE
THE TRADITIONAL LABOR MOVEMENT

Unions should also explore models developed by non-traditional worker organizations. The Coalition of Immokalee Workers (CIW), a worker-led human rights organization of farmworkers founded in 1993 in Immokalee, Florida, provides the most inspirational—and successful—model, a "radically different accountability mechanism."[33]

CIW operates in agriculture, an abusive and exploitative sector that functions through a series of farm labor contractors who wield immense power over workers' lives in an environment characterized by intimidation and terror.[34] Sexual abuse in the fields is pervasive: more than 80 percent of female Mexican American farmworkers have experienced some form of sexual harassment at work.[35] In cases brought by the U.S. Equal Employment Opportunity Commission, immigrant women shared stories of being forced to have sex with the hiring official at the beginning of harvest seasons, and of sexual assaults being so common that they described workplaces as "*fields de calzon*" or "fields of panties" or the "Green Motel" because women were raped there by supervisors.[36]

CIW's efforts around sexual harassment are a central part of a multi-layered groundbreaking initiative, the Fair Food Program (FFP). Launched in 2011 to improve working conditions for farmworkers, the FFP is a unique partnership among growers, farmworkers, and major food retailers. It operates through legally binding agreements between CIW and large retail companies. These companies pledge to purchase produce only from growers who adhere to the FFP's code of conduct, which includes substantial protections against sexual harassment.[37]

The FFP's comprehensive approach also includes worker-to-worker education: CIW runs live, interactive, peer-to-peer training that use theater, artwork, and real situations to teach workers about their rights. CIW has conducted more than 775 in-person sessions that have educated more than 60,000 workers across seven U.S. states.[38]

Another key element in the program's success is the Fair Food Standards Council (FFSC), which conducts regular audits of participating farms and investigates worker complaints, which they can file confidentially. The FFSC's in-depth audits—which, unlike more social responsibility audits, are not controlled or influenced by the corporations—include access to company records and on-site observations. "FFSC's investigators are local and have detailed knowledge of crews, side hand references, and supervisors' nicknames."

FFSC's enforcement mechanism fixes many of the hurdles that survivors face when they seek justice. "Victims of sexual harassment with physical contact don't have to prove that they were touched in an inappropriate place or that the perpetrator intended sexual gratification, as they would need to demonstrate in a legal case," according to Laura Espinoza, a retired judge who heads the FFSC.[39] The process is less formal and more responsive to the lives of workers. For example, justice is often fleeting for workers who move from state to state, as farmworkers do. "When necessary, FFSC has stayed in contact with complainants who have left the state. This doesn't happen in the legal system."[40] Importantly, FFSC always provides complainants with access to the civil or criminal justice systems, should they choose to pursue those. However, many workers—vindicated by FFSC's prompt, confidential investigations and consequences for abusers—choose not to.

"Workers have seen enough supervisors' heads roll for things that would never have even raised an eyebrow before—a slap on the butt, an arm on the shoulder. If a worker complained about that before, first of all, they'd be fired. Second, others would laugh. It's not a laughing matter anymore. Those days are over," said Espinoza.[41]

Since the Fair Food Program started in 2011, auditors say cases of sexual assault have been virtually eliminated on participating farms.[42]

"The program works because workers are empowered to monitor their own rights. This shifts the culture away from secrecy."[43] This is precisely the kind of shift that unions should be pushing for. Indeed, the USWW janitors got some of the inspiration for their own wonderful *promotora* model from discussions with CIW.[44]

By implementing the changes outlined above, unions would be well on their way to recognizing sexual harassment as universal collective harm, which by its nature merits the full attention of institutions that exist to protect workers' rights.

Notes

INTRODUCTION

1. Safran, C. (1976, November). What men do to women on the
    job: A shocking look at sexual harassment. *Redbook*, 148, 149.
    While it may seem odd that I'm citing a woman's magazine as
    a source of data, *Redbook*'s research is one of the two most-
    cited sources of data on the incidence of sexual harassment on
    the job. The other is a much smaller survey conducted in 1975
    by the Working Women United Institute, which found that 70
    percent of the 155 women who responded had been sexually
    harassed on the job.
2. *Ibid.*
3. Mateo, A., & Menza, K. (2017, March 27). The results of a 1976
    survey of women about sexual harassment at work remain vir-
    tually unchanged in 2017. *Redbook*.
4. Ryan, M. (2023). *Burn it down: Power, complicity, and a call for
    change in Hollywood*. Mariner Books, p. 271.
5. U.S. Equal Employment Opportunity Commission (2016).
    *Select Task Force on the Study of Harassment in the Work-
    place: Report of Co-Chairs Chai R. Feldblum & Victoria A.
    Lipnic*. When researchers ask whether a woman has been
    sexually harassed, the results skew towards the lower end of
    the spectrum; when researchers ask about specific behaviors
    that women experience, the results point to the higher end.
6. Eidelson, J. (2017, November 2). *SEIU ousts senior leaders for
    abusive behavior toward women*. Bloomberg.
7. American Federation of Teachers (2017, November 7). *AFT
    President Randi Weingarten on sexual harassment in the labor
    movement*.
8. Eidelson, J. (2017, November 7). *U.S. labor leaders confront
    sexual harassment in top ranks*. Bloomberg.

9. hooks, b. (2009). *Teaching critical thinking: Practical wisdom.* Routledge.

10. Peck, E. (2021, January 6). More former United Way employees say they experienced harassment, discrimination. Retrieved April 24, 2024, from www.huffpost.com/entry/united-way-former-employees-letter-harassment-discrimination_n_5f f5c73cc5b6ea7351c6fc72); Bowman, L. (2022). *Harasshole: A cautionary tale of my time at "America's favorite charity"* [Kindle edition]. Amplify Publishing.

11. United Way Worldwide (2021). *Form 990: Return of organization exempt from income tax.* Retrieved September 20, 2024, from https://s3.amazonaws.com/uww.assets/site/annual_report/2021/2021_United_Way_Worldwide_Form_990.pdf

12. Peck, E. (2020, November 20). United Way accused of retaliation against women employees. *Huffington Post.* Retrieved September 20, 2014, from www.huffpost.com/entry/united-way-retaliation-female-employees_n_5fb82c6 1c5b67493dd366529

13. Avendaño, A., & Seabrook, L. (2017, November 10). Top 10 things unions can do right now to address sexual harassment in the workplace. *OnLabor.* Retrieved Spril 24, 2024, from https://onlabor.org/top-10-things-unions-can-do-right-now-to-address-sexual-harassment-in-the-workplace/

14. International Labour Organization (n.d.). *Ratifications of C190—Violence and Harassment Convention, 2019 (No. 190).* NORMLEX Information System on International Labour Standards. Retrieved September 29, 2024, from https://normlex.ilo.org/dyn/normlex/en/f?p=1000:11300:0::NO:1130 0:P11300_INSTRUMENT_ID:3999810

1 IN THE COURSE OF HISTORY

1. Murolo, P., & Chitty, A.B. (2001). *From the folks who brought you the weekend: A short, illustrated history of labor in the United States.* New Press.

2. Foner, P.S. (1979). *Women and the labor movement: From colonial times to the eve of World War I.* Free Press.

3. Kessler-Harris, A. (1975). Where are the organized women? *Feminist Studies, 3*(1), 92–110.

4. *Ibid.*, p. 93.

5. Van Raaphorst, D. (1988). *Union maids not wanted.* Praeger.

6. Chaffe, W. (1972). *The American woman: Her changing social, economic and political roles.* Oxford University Press.

7. Kessler-Harris, 1975, p. 96.

8. Murolo & Chitty, 2001.

9. Balser, D. (1987), *Sisterhood & solidarity: Feminism and labor in modern times.* South End Press, p. 27.

10. Kessler-Harris, 1975, p. 97.

11. Novkov, J. (2001). *Constituting workers, protecting women: Gender, law, and labor in the Progressive Era and New Deal years.* University of Michigan Press.

12. *Frontiero v. Richardson*, 411 U.S. 677, 691 (1973) (Brennan, J., dissenting).

13. Kessler-Harris, A. (2001). *In pursuit of equity: Women, men, and the quest for economic citizenship in 20th-century America.* Oxford University Press.

14. Foner, 1979.

15. Deslippe, D.A. (2000). *Rights, not roses: Unions and the rise of working-class feminism, 1945–80.* University of Illinois Press.

16. Alimahomed-Wilson, J. (2016). *Solidarity forever? Race, gender, and unionism in the ports of Southern California.* Lexington Books, p. 158.

17. Crain, M. (2007). Sex discrimination as collective harm. In D.S. Cobble (Ed.), *The sex of class.* Cornell University Press, pp. 99–116.

18. Deslippe, 2000.

19. Institute for Women's Policy Research (2018). *The gender wage gap by occupation 2017 and by race and ethnicity.* Retrieved May 4, 2024, from https://iwpr.org/publications/gender-wage-gap-occupation- 2017-race-ethnicity/

20. Milkman, R. (2016). *On gender, labor, and inequality.* University of Illinois Press.

21. *Ibid.*

22. Baker, C.N. (2013). *The women's movement against sexual harassment.* Cambridge University Press.

23. Moore, M. (1996). *Women in the mines.* Twayne Publishers.

24. Sullivan, A.M. (1979, August). Women say no to sexual harassment. *Coal Age, 84,* 84.

25. M. Moore, 1996, p. 131.

26. Segrave, K. (1994). *The sexual harassment of women in the workplace 1600 to 1993.* McFarland & Co.

27. M. Moore, 1996, p. xliii.

28. Bingham, C., & Gansler, L.L. (2002). *Class action: The story of Lois Jenson and the landmark case that changed sexual harassment law.* Doubleday, p. 33.

29. *Ibid.,* p. 14.

30. *Ibid.,* p. 47.

31. *Ibid.,* p. 132.

32. Grimsley, K.D. (1996, October 27). A hostile workplace. *The Washington Post.*

33. *Ibid.,* p. 262.

34. *Ibid.*

35. M. Moore, 1996, p. 107.

36. *Ibid.,* p. 116.

37. *Ibid.,* p. 132.

38. Sullivan, 1979, p. 75.

39. Segrave, 1994, p. 97.

40. Goldberg, D., & Griffey, T. (2010). White male identity politics, the building trades, and the future of American labor. In D. Goldberg & T. Griffey (Eds.), *Black power at work: Community control, affirmative action, and the construction industry.* Cornell University Press, pp. 189–207.

41. LaTour, J. (2008). *Sisters in the brotherhoods: Working women organizing for equality in New York City.* Palgrave Macmillan, p. 26.

42. *Ibid.,* p. 26.

43. *Ibid.,* p 55.

44. *Ibid.,* p. 67.

45. *Ibid.,* p. 62.

46. Ybarra, M. (1991, April 30). Still a man's world: For women, the construction trades are proving to be a bastion of bias. *Los Angeles Times.*

47. Schroedel, J. (1985). *Alone in a crowd: Women in the trades tell their stories.* Temple University Press.

48. Ybarra, 1991.

49. LaTour, 2008, p. 173.

50. *Ibid.,* p. 175.

51. *Ibid,* p. 178.

52. Meyer, S. (2016). *Manhood on the line: Working class masculinities in the American heartland.* University of Illinois Press, p. 202.

53. *Ibid.,* p. 202.

54. *Ibid.,* p. 202.

55. Sharpe, R. (1996, July 10). Women at Mitsubishi say union fell short on sexual harassment. *Wall Street Journal.*

56. Foner, P.S. (1979). *Women and the labor movement: From colonial times to the eve of World War I.* Free Press, p. 559.

57. *Ibid.,* p. 357.

58. *Ibid.,* p. 357.

59. Moore, C. (1981). Confronting sexual harassment: Three women speak. *Tradeswomen: A Quarterly Magazine for Women in Blue-Collar Work, 1*(1), 9.

60. *Ibid.,* p. 13.

61. *Ibid.*

62. M. Moore, p. xxv.

63. Baker, 2013, p. 73.

64. *Ibid.,* p. 74

65. Crain, M. (1995). Women, labor unions, and hostile work environment sexual harassment: The untold story. *Texas Journal of Women and the Law, 4*(1), 9–82.

66. Chira, S., & Einhorn, C. (2017, December 19). How tough is it to change a culture of harassment? Ask women at Ford. *The New York Times.*

67. *Ibid.*

68. Settles, J. (2015, May 5). The UAW National Ford Department is aware of an active investigation regarding allegations of

sexual harassment at the Chicago Assembly Plant. [Facebook post]. Facebook. Retrieved December 19, 2019 from https://www.facebook.com/uawforddept/posts/838229052913131.

2   UNIONS UNDER THE #METOO SPOTLIGHT

1. *Clueless*, Directed by Amy Heckerling, Paramount Pictures (1995).
2. Strom, A. (2018). Sexual harassment and our undemocratic workplaces. *OnLabor*. Retrieved November 3, 2024, from https://onlabor.org/sexual-harassment-and-our-undemocratic-workplaces/
3. AFL-CIO website (cached).
4. National Academies of Sciences, Engineering, and Medicine (2018). *Sexual harassment of women: Climate, culture, and consequences in academic sciences, engineering, and medicine* (P.A. Johnson, S.E. Widnall, & F.F. Benya, Eds.). National Academies Press, p. 42.
5. Crain, M. (1995). Women, labor unions, and hostile work environment sexual harassment: The untold story. *Texas Journal of Women and the Law*, 4(1), 14.
6. Lange, A. (2018, June 6). "I'm sorry" is not enough: Inside the union trial of an alleged sexual harasser. *BuzzFeed News*. Retrieved November 3, 2024, from https://www.buzzfeednews.com/article/arianelange/chris-savino-animation-guild-metoo-allegations-nickelodeon
7. Goldberg, Lesley (2017, October 19). Nickelodeon fires "Loud House" createer after sexual harassment allegations. *The Hollywood Reporter*. Retrieved November 3, 2024, from www.hollywoodreporter.com/tv/tv-news/nickelodeon-fires-loud-house-creator-sexual-harassment-allegations-1050485/
8. *Ibid.*
9. Lange, 2018.
10. *Ibid.*
11. Amidi, A. (2018, May 30). The Animation Guild has suspended "The Loud House" creator Chris Savino. *Cartoon Brew*. Retrieved November 3, 2024, from www.cartoonbrew.com/

artist-rights/breaking-the-animation-guild-has-suspended-the-loud-house-creator-chris-savino-exclusive-158674.html

12. *Ibid.*

13. Spector, M. (2017, October). Harvey Weintein's crimes and SAG's failure, *Jacobin*; Ng, David (2018, February 1). Guild sets sexual harassment Policy. *Los Angeles Times*, C2.

14. Hampton, M. (2018). Hollywood's biggest union turned a blind eye to sexual abuse. *The Guardian*. Retrieved November 2024, from www.theguardian.com/commentisfree/2018/jan/18/hollywood-union-sexual-abuse

15. Kirshner, M. (2017). I was not protected from Harvey Weinstein. It's time for institutional change. *The Globe and Mail*. Retrieved November 3, 2024, from www.theglobeandmail.com/opinion/i-was-a-victim-of-harvey-weinstein-but-we-have-to-focus-on-the-future/article36584019/

16. *Ibid.*

17. Robb, D. (2017). SAG-AFTRA in legal quandary over expanding sex abuse scandal. *Deadline*. Retrieved November 3, 2024, from https://deadline.com/2017/11/hollywood-sex-abuse-scandals-sag-aftra-legal-quandary-email-1202207448/

18. *Ibid.*

19. Robb, D. (2015, June 5). SAG-AFTRA threatened to sue director Amy Berg over "An Open Secret". *Deadline*. Retrieved November 3, 2014, from https://deadline.com/2015/06/sag-aftra-threatening-sue-an-open-secret-director-amy-berg-1201438339/

20. *Ibid.*

21. Phung, A, & Melas, C. (2018, May 28). Women accuse Morgan Freeman of inappropriate behavior, harassment. *CNN*. Retrieved November 3, 2024, from www.cnn.com/2018/05/26/entertainment/morgan-freeman-harassment-statement/index.html

22. *Ibid.*

23. Handel, J. (2018, May 24). SAG-AFTRA reconsiders Morgan Freeman's Lifetime Achievent Award. *Hollywood Reporter*.

24. Robb, D. (2018, September 6). SAG-AFTRA won't rescind Morgan Freeman's Life Achievement Award after

investigating sex harassment claims. *Deadline*. Retrieved November 4, 2024, from https://deadline.com/2018/09/morgan-freeman-sag-lifetime-achievement-award-keeping-sag-aftra-investigation-harassment-1202458552/

25. SAG-AFTRA (n.d.). Four pillars of change initiative. *SAG-AFTRA*. Retrieved November 3, 2024, from https://www.sagaftra.org/contracts-industry-resources/report-discrimination/four-pillars-change-initiative/espa%C3%B1ol/four

26. *Ibid*.

27. McNary, D. (2019). SAG-AFTRA finds Kip Pardue guilty in sexual harassment case. *Variety*. Retrieved November 3, 2024, from https://variety.com/2019/tv/news/sag-aftra-kip-pardue-sexual-harassment-case-1203260707/

28. Patten, D. (2024, February 22). Intimacy coordinator rules tightened by SAG-AFTRA after off-set indiscretions. *Deadline*. Retrieved November 4, 2024, from https://deadline.com/2024/02/intimacy-coordinator-rules-tightened-sag-aftra-jenna-ortega-1235834577/; Yandoli, K.L. (2023, November 36). How Hollywood's sex sccenes will change with the new SAG-AFTRA contract. *Rolling Stone*.

29. Eidelson, J. (2017, November 17). U.S. labor leaders confront sexual harassment in their top ranks. *Bloomberg*.

30. Lewis, C. (2017, October 23). A top labor executive has resigned after complaints about his relationships with female staffers. *BuzzFeed News*; Eidelson, 2017.

31. Lewis, 2017. *Buzzfeed News*.

32. Lewis, C. (2017, October 19). A top labor executive has been suspended after complaints about his relationships with female staffers. *Buzzfeed News*.

33. Eidelson, J. (2017, November 2). SEIU ousts senior leaders for abusive behavior toward women. *Bloomberg*.

34. *Sturge v. SEIU United HEalthcare Workers West et al.*, Superior Court of California, County of Alameda, Case Number RG18905355, filed July 10, 2018.

35. Written Questions for Nicole Berner, Nominee to be United States Circuit Judge for the Fourth Circuit, Senator Richard

Durbin, Chair, Senate Judiciary Committee, December 20, 2023; Exhibit A, Plaintff's Opposition to SEIU-UHW's Motion for Summary Adjudication of Issues (November 25, 2019) (On file with author).

36. Keiper, A. (2020, January 29). SEIU branch settles sexual-assault lawsuit, overhauls internal reporting policies. *Fox News*.

37. Exhibit A, Plaintff's Opposition to SEIU-UHW's Motion for Summary Adjudication of Issues.

38. *Ibid.*

39. Written Questions for Nicole Berner, Nominee to be United States Circuit Judge for the Fourth Circuit, Senator Richard Durbnin, Chair, Senate Judiciary Committee, December 20, 2023.

40. Debra Katz joins SEIU Advisory Board (2017, November 3). *Katz, Banks Kumin*. Retrieved November 3, 2024, from https://katzbanks.com/news/debra-katz-joins-seiu-advisory-board/

3 THE SURVIVORS

1. S. Wilder, personal communication, March 13, 2024.

2. S. Wilder, personal communication.

3. United Steelworkers (n.d.). Women of steel. Retrieved April 26, 2024, from https://m.usw.org/act/activism/women-of-steel

4. R. Kabir, personal communication, October 24, 2023–May 9, 2024.

5. Yang, J. (2020). Report of the independent investigation into allegations of harassment and related misconduct against J. David Cox. *Working IDEAL*, p. 4.

6. R. Kabir personal communication.

7. Yang, 2020, p. 14.

8. *Ibid*, p. 13.

9. *Ibid.*

10. *Ibid.*

11. *Ibid.*, p. 14.

12. Yang, 2020, p. 14.

13. Eidelson, J. (2019, October 28). AFGE president accused of sexual harassment in #MeToo scandal. *Bloomberg*. Retrieved

April 27, 2024, from https://m.usw.org/act/activism/women-of-steel

www.bloomberg.com/news/articles/2019-10-28/afge-president-accused-of-sexual-harassment-in-metoo-scandal

14. *Ibid.*

15. Yang, 2020, p. 1.

16. R. Kabir, personal communication.

17. Yang, 2020, p. 28.

18. *Ibid.*

19. *Ibid.*, p. 17.

20. Eidelson, 2019.

21. Yang, 2020, pp. 17–18.

22. *Ibid.*, pp. 22, 30.

23. *Ibid.*, p. 30.

24. *Rife v. American Federation of Labor and Congress of Industrial Organizations*, No. 23-cv-01884 (M.D. Pa. filed November 13, 2023).

25. Eidelson, J. (2022, April 14). Top Pennsylvania state AFL-CIO officer accused of misconduct. *Bloomberg.* Retrieved April 27, 2024, from https://m.usw.org/act/activism/women-of-steel www.bloomberg.com/news/articles/2022-04-14/top-pennsylvania-state-afl-cio-officer-accused-of-misconduct

26. *Rife v. American Federation of Labor and Congress of Industrial Organizations*, 2023, para. 64.

27. *Ibid.*, para. 69, 70.

28. R. Rife, personal communication, February 2023–May 2024.

29. *Rife v. UFCW Local 1776*, No. 202102348 (Pa. Human Relations Commn filed May 11, 2022).

30. UFCW Local 1776, Answer, *Rife v. UFCW Local 1776*, No. 202102348 (Pa. Human Relations Comm'n filed June 15, 2022).

31. *Ibid.*, para. 12.

32. *Ibid.*, para. 9.

33. Eidelson, 2022.

34. *Ibid.*

35. *Ibid.*

36. *Ibid.*

37. *Rife v. UFCW Local 1776.* She and two of her former coworkers are also suing the Pennsylvania AFL-CIO and the national
AFL-CIO in federal court. On July 29, 2024, the court denied
defendants' attempt to dismiss the case. *Rife v. AFL-CIO*, No.
23-cv-01884 (M.D. Pa. July 29, 2024).

38. *Rife v. UFCW Local 1776*, para. 13; UFCW Local 1776, Answer,
Rife v. UFCW Local 1776, para.13.

39. *Rife v. UFCW Local 1776* para 8, 17; Rife, personal
communication.

40. UFCW Local 1776, Answer, *Rife v. UFCW Local 1776.*

41. *Ibid.*, para. 7.A, 12.

42. Rife, personal communication.

43. Valentina is not her real name.

44. Valentina, personal communication, March, 2019-April, 2024.

45. Christl, M.-E., Pham, K.-C.T., Rosenthal, A., & DePrince, A.P.
(2024). When institutions harm those who depend on them: A
scoping review of institutional betrayal. *Trauma, Violence, &
Abuse*, 1–17.

4   THE ENABLERS: LAW AND CULTURE

1. Safran, C. (1976). What men do to women on the job: A
shocking look at sexual harassment. *Redbook.*

2. Williams, J., Short, J., Brooks, M., Hardcastle, H., Ellis, T., &
Saron, R. (2019). What's reasonable now? Sexual harassment
law after the norm cascade. *Texas Law Review.*

3. Amanpour, C. (2017, November 15). [Remarks at the Committee to Protect Journalists International Press Freedom
Awards gala]. (On file with the author).

4. U.S. Equal Employment Opportunity Commission (2016).
*Select Task Force on the Study of Harassment in the Workplace:
Report of Co-Chairs Chai R. Feldblum & Victoria A. Lipnic.*

5. Yang, J. (2020). Report of the independent investigation into
allegations of harassment and related misconduct against
J. David Cox. Working IDEAL, p. 7.

6. *Ibid.*, p. 30.

7. National Academies of Sciences, Engineering, and Medicine (2018). *Sexual harassment of women: Climate, culture, and consequences in academic sciences, engineering, and medicine* (P.A. Johnson, S.E. Widnall, & F.F. Benya, Eds.). National Academies Press, p. 121.

8. Coleman, J. (2013, May 6). Six components of a great corporate culture. *Harvard Business Review*; *ibid.*, p. 124.

9. By culture, I refer to the invisible norms that dictate who is valued, what matters, and how resources are allocated. As in any organization, union culture does not exist in isolation: it shapes how unions function, sets priorities, and responds to issues that challenge established norms.

10. Crain, M., & Matheny, K. (1999). Labor;s divided ranks: Privilege and the united front ideology. *Cornell Law Review, 84*(6), 1542–626.

11. Farley, L. (1978). *Sexual shake-down: The sexual harassment of women on the job*. McGraw Hill, p. 157.

12. Needleman, R. (1993). Comments. In D.D. Cobble (Ed.), *Women and unions: Forging a partnership*. ILR Press, pp. 406–9.

13. Hill, H. (1959, December 1). Labor unions and the Negro: The record of discrimination. *Commentary*.

14. Crain, M. (1995). Women, labor unions, and hostile work environment sexual harassment: The untold story. *Texas Journal of Women and the Law*, 4(1).

15. Cohen, Arb. (1982). Anaconda Copper Co. *Bureau of National Affairs Labor Arbitration Reports, 78*, 690.

16. Greg is the grievant in this case.

17. National Academy of Arbitrators (2022, April 7). *NAA L&E Arbitration Awards*. 2022 NAA Lexis 9.

18. *Ibid.*, p. 6.

19. *Ibid.*, p. 13.

20. *Ibid.*, p. 8.

21. *Ibid.*, p. 7.

22. *Ibid.*, p.13.

23. National Labor Relations Board (1975). Dreis & Krump Mfg. *National Labor Relations Board Decisions, 221*, 309–15.

24. *Ibid.*, p. 310.

25. Shearer, Arb. (1988). Cante Industries. *Bureau of National Affairs Labor Arbitration Reports*, *90*, 1230.

26. Crain, 1995.

27. *Ibid.*

28. The arbitrator rejected the defense, but nonetheless reduced the penalty from discharge to a ten-day suspension without pay. Viani, Arb. (2022). International Brotherhood of Teamsters. *Bureau of National Affairs Labor Arbitration Reports*, 237.

29. United States Court of Appeals, Seventh Circuit (1976). Advance Industries Division-Overhead Door Corp. v. National Labor Relations Board. *Federal Reporter, 2d Series*, *540*, 878–82.

30. National Labor Relations Board (1989). Calliope Designs. *National Labor Relations Board Decisions*, *297*, 510.

31. *Ibid.*

32. National Labor Relations Board (1989). Gloversville Embossing Corp. *National Labor Relations Board Decisions*, *297*, 182.

33. National Labor Relations Board. (2023). Hood River Distillers, Inc. *National Labor Relations Board Decisions*, *372*, No. 126.

34. Of course, these doctrines and practices also harm any worker who is not a cis white male.

35. National Academies of Sciences, Engineering, and Medicine, 2018.

36. Alleyne, R. (1999). Arbitrating sexual harassment grievances: A representation dilemma for unions. *University of Pennsylvania Journal of Labor and Employment Law*, *2*(1), 1–52.

37. Chira, S., & Einhorn, C. (2017, December 19). How tough is it to change a culture of harassment? Ask women at Ford. *The New York Times*.

38. Hickox, S.A., & Kaminski, M. (2019). Measuring arbitration's effectiveness in addressing workplace harassment. *Hofstra Labor & Employment Law Journal*, *36*(2), 293–352.

39. This duty is a legal obligation derived from the structure of labor law, which is based on a system of majority rule and exclusive representation. In 1944, the U.S. Supreme Court imposed on unions an obligation to represent all members of the bargaining unit, even if some members might disagree

with the union's positions. Supreme Court of the United States (1944). Steele v. Louisville & Nashville Railway Co. *United States Reports, 323*, 192–208.

40. Crain & Matheny, 1999.

41. Supreme Court of the United States (1998). Marquez v. Screen Actors Guild. *United States Reports, 525*, 33–59.

42. United States Court of Appeals, Eighth Circuit (1980). Smith v. Hussmann Refrigerator Co. *Federal Reporter, 2d Series, 619*, 1229–46.

43. United States District Court, Eastern District of Missouri (1998). Equal Employment Opportunity Commission v. General Motors Corp. *Federal Supplement, 2d Series, 11*, 1077–9.

44. U.S. Equal Employment Opportunity Commission, 2016.

45. Gerstein, T. (2017, December 6). Sexual harassment: New laws that would help. *OnLabor*. Retrieved May 4, 2024, from https://onlabor.org/sexual-harassment-new-laws-that-would-help/

46. National Labor Relations Board (2020). General Motors, LLC. *National Labor Relations Board Decisions, 369*, No. 127 & National Labor Relations Board (2020). General Motors LLC and Charles Robinson. *National Labor Relations Board Decisions, 369*, No. 127. Those cases involved the use of profanity and racist language in the workplace during the exercise of conduct otherwise protected by the National Labor Relations Act (NLRA).

47. American Federation of Labor and Congress of Industrial Organizations (2020). Brief of the American Federation of Labor and Congress of Industrial Organizations as Amicus Curiae. In *General Motors, LLC and Charles Robinson* (NLRB Cases Nos. 14-CA-197985 and 14-CA-208242). National Labor Relations Board.

48. National Labor Relations Board (2014). Fresh & Easy Neighborhood Market, Inc. *National Labor Relations Board Decisions, 361*, 151.

49. National Labor Relations Board (2004). Holling Press, Inc. *National Labor Relations Board Decisions, 343*, 301–2.

50. Healy, G., & Kirton, G. (2024). Women's long-term social movement participation—an American case. In G. Healy & G. Kirton (Eds.), *Gender and leadership: Research and practice*. Edward Elgar Publishing, pp. 242–56.

51. International Labour Organization (2020). *Empowering women at work: Trade union policies and practices.*

52. Institute for Women's Policy Research (n.d.). Status of women in the States. *Women in Unions*. Retrieved November 3, 2024, from https://statusofwomendata.org/women-in-unions/

53. Politico (2024, May 24). How women are changing labor unions. *Women Rule*. Retrieved November 3, 2024, from www.politico.com/newsletters/women-rule/2024/05/24/how-women-are-changing-labor-unions-00159882

54. Cobble, D.S. (2012). *Gender equality and labor movements: Toward a global perspective*. Solidarity Center.

55. *Ibid.*, p. 41.

5   RAYS OF HOPE

1. Schwartz, M. (1990, July 31). AFL-CIO takes no position on abortion. *The Washington Post.*

2. American Federation of Labor–Congress of Industrial Organizations (2012, March 14). Statement on women's access to quality and affordable reproductive health care. *AFL-CIO*. Retrieved November 3, 2024, from https://aflcio.org/about/leadership/statements/statement-womens-access-quality-and-affordable-reproductive-health-care

3. American Federation of Labor–Congress of Industrial Organizations (n.d.). Reproductive rights are worker rights. Retrieved November 3, 2024, from https://aflcio.org/reproductive-rights

4. Eidelson, J. (2013, January 29). Alt-labor. *The American Prospect.*

5. Valles, A. (2018, October 31). *Written testimony of Alejandra Valles Secretary-Treasurer of SEIU United Service Workers West (USWW)* [Testimony]. U.S. Equal Employment Opportunity Commission.

6. West, Z., Pinto, S., & Wagner, K.C. (2020). *Sweeping change: Building survivor and worker leadership to confront sexual harassment in the janitorial industry.* ILR Worker Institute.

7. *Ibid.,* p. 12.

8. Ziskin, L. (Executive Producer) (2015). *Rape on the night shift* [Television series episode]. In *Frontline.* PBS.

9. West et al., 2020, p. 12.

10. Valles, 2018.

11. S. Diaz & A. Valles, personal communication, June 14, 2019.

12. A. Valles personal communication, September 20, 2021–April, 2024.

13. *Ibid.*

14. S. Diaz, personal communication.

15. A. Valles, personal communication.

16. *Ibid.*

17. West et al., 2020, p. 12.

18. *Ibid.,* p. 11.

19. A. Valles & S. Diaz, personal communication.

20. *Ibid.*

21. A. Valles, personal communication.

22. West et al., 2020.

23. Pinto, S., West, Z., & Wagner, K.C. (2021). Healing into power: An approach for confronting workplace sexual violence. *New Labor Forum.*

24. Maria, personal communication, 2019.

25. Cal. Assemb. AB-547 (2019-2020). Reg. Sess. (Cal. 2019); West et al.., 2020, p. 14.

26. A. Valles, personal communication.

27. *Ibid.*

28. West et al., 2020, p. 14.

29. *Ibid.,* p. 11.

30. United Service Workers West (2012). United Service Workers West Northern California Maintenance Contractors Agreement [USWW NC MCA], 2012-2016, Appendix G.

31. Kamper, D. (2023, March 22). What's fueling the graduate worker union upsurge? *Labor Notes.* Retrieved November 3,

2024, from https://labornotes.org/2023/03/whats-fueling-graduate-worker-union-upsurge

32. Ilies, R., Hauserman, N., Schwochau, S., & Stibal, J. (2003). Reported incidence rates of work-related sexual harassment in the United States: Using meta-analysis to explain reported rate disparities. *Personnel Psychology*, 56(3), 607–31.

33. Association of American Universities (2019, October 15). *AAU Campus Climate Survey (2019)*. Retrieved May 10, 2024, from www.aau.edu/key-issues/campus-climate-and-safety/aau-campus-climate-survey-2019

34. Kelsky, K. (2017). *Sexual harassment in the academy: A crowdsource survey. The Professor Is In*. Retrieved May 10, 2024, from https://theprofessorisin.com/metoophd-sexual-harassment-in-the-academy-survey/

35. O'Callaghan, E., Shepp, V., Kirkner, A., & Lorenz, K. (2021). Sexual harassment in the academy: Harnessing the growing labor movement in higher education to address sexual harassment against graduate students. *Violence Against Women*, 27(5), 575–97.

36. Duwaji, O. (2024, March 28). High fees paid by international students help US universities balance their books. *The World*.

37. Harvard University (2015). Table 1. In *Report on the AAU Campus Climate Survey on Sexual Assault and Sexual Misconduct*.

38. Phipps, A. (2020). Reckoning up: Sexual harassment and violence in the neoliberal university. *Gender and Education*, 32(2), 227–43.

39. *Ibid.*, p. 229.

40. Yumusak, E. (2020, June 24). #MeToo's strike test: The Harvard Graduate Union and the limits of Time's Up organizing. *The Drift*, 1.

41. *Ibid.*.

42. Vedder, R. (2018, April 8). There are really almost no truly private universities. *Forbes*. Retrieved June 10, 2024, from www.forbes.com/sites/richardvedder/2018/04/08/there-are-really-almost-no-truly-private-universities/?sh=4af77d0d57bc

43. Yumusak, 2020.

44. *Ibid.*

45. Gibbons, A. (2021, June 10). Harvard bans former anthropology chair after finding persistent sexual harassment. *Science.*

46. Ahmed, S. (2021). *Complaint!* Duke University Press.

47. Yumusak, 2020.

48. Kim, A.H., & Xu, M. (2022, May 26). "An open secret": Harvard graduate students decry harassment, neglect from faculty. *The Harvard Crimson.* Retrieved June 10, 2024, from www.thecrimson.com/article/2022/5/26/graduate-students-power-dynamics/

49. Harvard Graduate Student Union-UAW (2020). Times Up Committee. Retrieved June 10, 2024, from https://harvardgradunion.org/times-up-committee/

50. Yumusak, 2020.

51. MIT Graduate Student Union (2023). Article 10: Nondiscrimination. In *2023–2026 Contract.* Retrieved November 3, 2024, from https://mitgsu.org/cba/article-10

52. Lynes, C. (2022, October 17). A history of grad student labor unions: Private universities see explosion in unionization efforts. *The Brown Daily Herald.* Retrieved June 10, 2024, from www.browndailyherald.com/article/2022/10/a-history-of-grad-student-labor-unions

53. *Ibid.*

54. Yumusak, E. (2023, March). Lessons from Region 9A for real recourse [Unpublished] (On file with the author).

55. *Ibid.*

56. *Ibid.*

57. *Ibid.*

58. Ahmed, 2021, p. 340.

59. Jacobs, J. (2018, November 11). Hotels see panic buttons as a #MeToo solution for workers. Guest bans? Not so fast. *The New York Times.*

60. Lyons, S. (2018). "Hands off pants on": The collective and radical art of shedding self-doubt. *Labor Studies Journal, 43*(4), 263–8.

61. Alimahomed-Wilson, J. (2016). *Solidarity forever? Race, gender, and unionism in the ports of Southern California.* Lexington Books.

62. J. Monti, personal communication, June 2020–October 2023.
63. *Ibid.*
64. Cooper, M. (2018, December 16). New York Philharmonic dismisses 2 players for unspecified misconduct. *The New York Times.*
65. Woolfe, Z. (2020, April 7). Philharmonic players, fired on misconduct grounds, are reinstated. *The New York Times.*
66. Sussman, S. (2024, April 12). A hidden sexual assault scandal at the New York Philharmonic. *Vulture.* Retrieved Novenmber 4, 2024, from www.vulture.com/article/new-york-philharmonic-sexual-assault-scandal.html
67. *Ibid.*
68. *Ibid.*
69. *Ibid.*
70. *Ibid.*
71. *Ibid.*
72. Hernandez, J. (2024, April 15). Philharmonic sidelines 2 players it tried to fire for misconduct. *The New York Times.*
73. *Ibid.*
74. Cutler, S. (2024, May). A heavy heart. *Allegro.* Retrieved November 3, 2024, from www.local802afm.org/allegro/articles/presidents-report-may-2024/
75. AFM Observer (2024, May 3). Strange guy in a strange union. Retrieved November 3, 2024, from https://theafmobserver.typepad.com/

6   THE GLOBAL RESPONSE

1. Strum, L. (2017, October 25). Twitter chat: What #MeToo says about sexual abuse in society. *PBS NewsHour.* Retrieved June 15, 2024, from www.pbs.org/newshour/nation/twitter-chat-what-metoo-says-about-sexual-abuse-in-society
2. Fox, K., & Diehm, J. (2017, November 9). #MeToo's global moment: The anatomy of a viral campaign. *CNN.* Retrieved June 15, 2024, from www.cnn.com/2017/11/09/world/metoo-hashtag-global-movement/index.html
3. *Ibid.*

4. Heymann, J., Moreno, G., Raub, A., & Sprague, A. (2022). Progress towards ending sexual harassment at work? A comparison of sexual harassment policy in 192 countries. *Journal of Comparative Policy Analysis: Research and Practice*, 25(2), 172–93.

5. International Labour Organization (2022). *Experiences of violence and harassment at work: A global first survey.*

6. *Ibid.*, p. 8.

7. World Policy Analysis Center (2017). *Preventing gender-based workplace discrimination and sexual harassment: New data on 193 countries.* UCLA Fielding School of Public Health.

8. International Labour Organization (2019). *Violence and Harassment Convention, 2019 (No. 190).*

9. *Ibid.*, Article 4.

10. Heap, L.S. (2023). *Preventing gender-based violence and harassment at work: A study of the potential of new regulatory approaches* [Unpublished doctoral dissertation]. RMIT University.

11. U.S. Department of Labor (2022, May 11). *The connection between unions and worker safety.* Retrieved June 15, 2024, from https://blog.dol.gov/2022/05/11/the-connection-between-unions-and-worker-safety

12. IndustriALL Global Union (2020, June 18). *The role of Uruguayan unions in the ratification of C190.* Retrieved June 15, 2024, from www.industriall-union.org/the-role-of-uruguayan-unions-in-the-ratification-of-c190

13. Trades Union Congress. (n.d.) *Tackling and preventing sexual harassment.* Retrieved June 15, 2024, from www.tuc.org.uk/sexualharassmentworkinggroup

14. N. Pound, personal communication, March 26, 2024.

15. Trades Union Congress (2021, November). *Preventing sexual harassment: A safer workplaces checklist for union reps.*

16. N. Pound, personal communication.

17. Horton, T. (2021). Musicians' Union calls for action on sexual harassment and abuse. *Press Association Mediapoint.*

18. Hind, K. (2022). First woman to run the Musicians' Union says she has received hundreds of sexual harassment and bullying

claims from women in the music industry. *MailOnline*. Retrieved November 4, 2024, from www.dailymail.co.uk/news/article-10656177/First-woman-run-Musicians-Union-says-received-hundreds-abuse-testimonies.html

19. *The Guardian* (2020, April 28). GMB boss Tim Roache resigns suddenly with health issues cited. Retrieved November 4, 2024, from www.theguardian.com/politics/2020/apr/28/gmb-boss-tim-roache-resigns-suddenly-with-health-issues-cited

20. England, C. (2020, May 1). Tim Roache resigned amid allegations of sexual assault, cover up and a "casting couch" culture at GMB. *Novara Media*.

21. Monaghan, K. (2020). Investigation into sexual harassment and the management of sexual harassment complaints within the GMB [Unpublished report]. Para. 116.

22. *Id.*, para. 122.

23. *The Herald* (2024, March 17). GMB's Gary Smith urged to apologise for "shooting match" comments. Retrieved November 4, 2024, from www.heraldscotland.com/news/24190973.gmbs-gary-smith-urged-apologise-shooting-match-comments/

24. Rodger, H. (2024, March 24). GMB union accused of silencing staff who complain of abuse in workplace. *Daily Record*. Retrieved November 4, 2024, from www.dailyrecord.co.uk/news/gmb-union-using-gagging-orders-32425770

25. ReelNews (2023, March 15). *#MeTU: TSSA General Secretary faces sexual harassment allegations* [Video]. YouTube. Retrieved November 4, 2024, from https://youtu.be/VennaJGXnJY

26. Transport Salaried Staffs' Association (2023, February 8). Independent inquiry report published. Retrieved November 4, 2024, from www.tssa.org.uk/news-and-events/tssa-news/independent-inquiry-report-published

27. ReelNews (2023, March 15). *#MeTU: Sexual harassment and violence in the trade union movement* [Video]. YouTube. Retrieved November 4, 2024, from www.youtube.com/watch?v=y63s5abAm1s

28. meTU Women (n.d.). *meTU Women* [Twitter account]. Twitter. Retrieved November 4, 2024, from https://twitter.com/meTUwomen

29. International Trade Union Confederation (2021, June 24). *Facilitator guide: Train the trainers toolkit on the ILO Violence and Harassment Convention (No. 190) and Recommendation (No. 206).*

30. Tshoaedi, M. (2017). The politics of male power and privilege in trade unions: Understanding sexual harassment in COSATU. In A. Bezuidenhout & M. Tshoaedi (Eds.), *Labour beyond COSATU: Mapping the rupture in South Africa's labour landscape.* Wits University Press, p. 131.

31. Briskin, L., & McDermott, P. (1993). Introduction. In L. Briskin & P. McDermott (Eds.), *Women challenging unions: Feminism, democracy, and militancy.* University of Toronto Press, p. 7.

32. Ledwith, S., & Munakamwe, J. (2015). Gender, union leadership and collective bargaining: Brazil and South Africa. *The Economic and Labour Relations Review, 26*(3), 415–29; Qu, X., Hui, C., Jing, F., Zijan, W., Zhenyu, N., & Yong, G. (2023). The prevalence of sexual violence against African women: A systematic review and meta-analysis. *African Health Sciences, 23*(3), 117–27.

33. Tshoaedi, 2017, p. 129.

34. *Ibid.*

35. Congress of South African Trade Unions (2022, September 28). COSATU statement on the alleged rape incident implicating a Congress delegate. *MediaDon.* Retrieved November 4, 2024, from https://mediadon.co.za/2022/09/28/cosatu-statement-on-the-alleged-rape-incident-implicating-a-congress-delegate/

36. Tshoaedi, 2017, p. 134.

37. *Ibid.*, p. 135.

38. *Ibid.*, p. 136.

39. Rütters, P. (2003). A brief look at the history of the Food Workers' International. In P. Rütters & R. Zimmermann (Eds.), *On the history and policy of the IUF.* Bibliothek der Friedrich-Ebert-Stiftung, pp. 11–32.

40. International Union of Food, Agricultural, Hotel, Restaurant, Catering, Tobacco and Allied Workers' Associations (n.d.).

Affiliates. Retrieved September 27, 2024, from www.iuf.org/who-we-are/affiliates/

41. B. Budin, personal communication, June 3, 2024.
42. Grune, J.A. (1989). Working women & the Food Secretariat. *Labor Research Review, 1*(13), 43–6.
43. Budin, personal communication.
44. International Labour Organization (2010). *Code of practice on safety and health in agriculture* (Section 19.5.3).
45. *Ibid.*, p. 203.
46. Yeung, B., & Cediel, A. (2013). Migration: Rape in the fields. *Berkeley Review of Latin American Studies*, Fall, 25–30.
47. Budin, personal communication.
48. Article 19 of the Convention requires that "Workers shall have access to adequate sanitary and washing facilities, installed and maintained in accordance with national laws and practice."
49. International Union of Food, Agricultural, Hotel, Restaurant, Catering, Tobacco and Allied Workers' Associations (n.d.). *IUF policy on sexual harassment*. Retrieved November 4, 2024, from https://pre2010.iuf.org/cgi-bin/dbman/db.cgi?db=default&ww=1&uid=default&ID=111&view_records=1&en=1

7 CHANGE IS ESSENTIAL

1. American Federation of State, County and Municipal Employees (AFSCME) (2018). Preventing and combating sexual harassment in the workplace. *AFSCME at Work*. Retrieved August 30, 2024, from https://afscmeatwork.org/harassment-conversation/preventing-and-combating-sexual-harassment-workplace
2. *Ibid.*
3. Lee, J. (2017, December 5). Broadway confronts casting couch. *Daily Labor Report (BNA), 232*, 8.
4. Schultz, V. (2001). Sex is the least of it: Let's focus law on work, not sex. In L. LeMoncheck & J. Sterba (Eds.), *Sexual harassment: Issues and answers*. Oxford University Press, p. 272.
5. AFL-CIO, 2018.

6. United States District Court, Eastern District of Missouri, 1998.

7. AFSCME, 2018, 34:05-36:00.

8. Bingham, C., & Gansler, L.L. (2002). *Class action: The story of Lois Jenson and the landmark case that changed sexual harassment law*. Doubleday, p. 14.

9. *Tradeswomen*: A quarterly magazine for women in blue-collar work (1993). *Tradeswomen, 8*(1).

10. National Academies of Sciences, Engineering, and Medicine (2018). *Sexual harassment of women: Climate, culture, and consequences in academic sciences, engineering, and medicine* (P.A. Johnson, S.E. Widnall, & F.F. Benya, Eds.). National Academies Press.

11. *Ibid*. This concept is adopted in the definition of "hostile environment" sexual harassment under the United Kingdom's 2010 Equality Act. Equality Act, 2010, c. 15 § 26 (UK).

12. Roxanne Rife, personal communication.

13. National Academies of Sciences, Engineering, and Medicine, 2018, p. 121.

14. Restaurant Opportunities Centers United (2014, October 7). The glass floor: Sexual harassment in the restaurant industry.

15. I reference that resolution only to show that the AFL-CIO has the ability to adopt such measures. Unfortunately, the organization has not released any data that it has collected on this topic.

16. Rubenstein-Heller, R. (n.d.). *The women of summer* [Doctoral dissertation, Bryn Mawr College]. Scholarship, Research, and Creative Work at Bryn Mawr College. Retrieved August 30, 2024, from https://repository.brynmawr.edu

17. For an example, see Midwest School for Women Workers (2021, June 2–24). The Polk School [Event]. University of Illinois at Chicago. Retrieved August 30, 2024, from www.facebook.com/midwestwomenworkers/photos/a.1389745227912702/2852392148314662/

18. Women's Institute for Leadership Development (n.d.). About WILD. Retrieved August 30, 2024, from http://wildlabor.org/about-wild/

19. Pinto, S., West, Z., & Wagner, K.C. (2021). Healing into power: An approach for confronting workplace sexual violence. *New Labor Forum*.

20. American Federation of Labor and Congress of Industrial Organizations (2018). Culture change training: Addressing unwanted behaviors in our movement. Retrieved August 30, 2024, from https://aflcio.org/sites/default/files/2024-02/Culturetraining.pdf

21. Downey, J. (2019, September 30). [Letter to Colleen Johnson] (Copy in possession of the author).

22. Shanley, P. (2018, July 30). Stephen Colbert says Leslie Moonves is "my guy," but stresses accountability. *The Hollywood Reporter*. Retrieved October 31, 2024, from www.hollywoodreporter.com/tv/tv-news/stephen-colbert-leslie-moonves-is-my-guy-but-stresses-accountability-1130332/

23. This scenario is based on a 2021 arbitration decision, 2021 AAA Lexis 305 (2021, April 6).

24. Goldscheid, J. (2021). #MeToo, sexual harassment and accountability: Considering the role of restorative approaches. *Ohio State Journal on Dispute Resolution*, 36(5), 689–736.

25. Balser, D. (1999). *Sisterhood and solidarity: Feminism and labor in modern times*. South End Press.

26. Lorde, A. (1981). The master's tools will never dismantle the master's house. In C. Moraga & G. Anzaldúa (Eds.), *This bridge called my back: Writings by radical women of color*. Persephone Press, pp. 94–7.

27. Oxfam America (n.d.). Safeguarding. Retrieved October 31, 2024, from www.oxfamamerica.org/explore/about-oxfam/safeguarding/

28. Finlay, K. (2023, April 19). Time to ban non-disclosure agreements: Ottawa has ignored the toxic sting of NDAs in cases of gender violence and sexual harassment. MPs and senators should put an end to their use now. *Policy Options*.

29. National Women's Law Center (2023). 2023 #MeToo workplace anti-harassment reforms. Retrieved October 31, 2024, from https://nwlc.org/wp-content/uploads/2023/09/2023_nwlc MeToo_Report-1.pdf

30. National Labor Relations Board (2023, February 21). Board rules that employers may not offer severance agreements requiring employees to broadly waive labor law rights. Retrieved October 31, 2024, from www.nlrb.gov/news-outreach/news-story/board-rules-that-employers-may-not-offer-severance-agreements-requiring

31. Olivier, I. (2021, July 26). Media unions are challenging the use of NDAs: Workers in the industry argue that nondisclosure agreements are a matter of workplace safety, making them "mandatory subjects of bargaining." *The Nation*.

32. Rodger, H. (2024). GMB union accused of silencing staff who complain of abuse in the workplace. *Daily Mail*. Retrieved September 16, 2024, from https://www.dailyrecord.co.uk/news/gmb-union-using-gagging-orders-32425770

33. U.S. Equal Employment Opportunity Commission, 2016.

34. Chang, V. (2020, March 9). After #MeToo, this group has nearly erased sexual harassment in farm fields. *Civil Eats*.

35. Graddy-Lovelace, G., & Jacobs, A. (2023, April 24). Sexual violence is a pervasive threat for female farm workers—here's how the US could reduce their risk. *The Conversation*. Retrieved October 31, 2024, from https://theconversation.com/sexual-violence-is-a-pervasive-threat-for-female-farm-workers-heres-how-the-us-could-reduce-their-risk-204871

36. Tamayo, W.R. (2009). The EEOC and immigrant workers. *University of San Francisco Law Review*, 44(2), 253–64.

37. Fair Food Standards Council (n.d.). Fair Food Code of Conduct. Retrieved October 31, 2024, from www.fairfoodstandards.org/resources/fair-food-code-of-conduct/

38. Asbed, G., & Hitov, S. (2017). Preventing forced labor in corporate supply chains: The fair food program and worker-driven social responsibility. *Wake Forest Law Review*, 52(2), 497–532.

39. Chang, 2020.

40. *Ibid.*

41. *Ibid.*

42. Asbed & Hitov, 2017.

43. Chang, 2020.

44. A. Valles, personal communication.

Index

The Pluto Press Newsletter

Hello friend of Pluto!

Want to stay on top of the best radical books
we publish?

Then sign up to be the first to hear about our
new books, as well as special events,
podcasts and videos.

You'll also get 50% off your first order with us
when you sign up.

Come and join us!

Go to bit.ly/PlutoNewsletter

Thanks to our Patreon subscriber:

Ciaran Kane

Who has shown generosity and
comradeship in support of our publishing.